WEBSTER'S
UNIVERSAL

BUSINESS
DICTIONARY

WEBSTER'S
UNIVERSAL

BUSINESS
DICTIONARY

**GEDDES&
GROSSET**

Published 2004 by Geddes & Grosset, David Dale House,
New Lanark, ML11 9DJ, Scotland

Copyright © 2004 Geddes & Grosset

ISBN 1 84205 445 7

Printed and bound in Canada

A

abandonment option a facility that allows an investor to terminate an investment sooner than originally agreed.

above-the-line 1 referring to those entries that appear above a horizontal line in a PROFIT AND LOSS ACCOUNT, which divides the entries that establish the profit or loss that has been achieved by the company from the entries that indicate how the profit is distributed. **2** referring to expenditure on mass media promotion or advertising, especially that which involves the payment of commission to an advertising agency. *See* BELOW-THE-LINE.

absolute cost advantage an advantage enjoyed by a country that enables it to produce certain goods more cheaply than others. Such advantages include a plentiful local supply of raw materials, cheap energy, low labor costs, etc.

absolute priority in BANKRUPTCY, the most important CREDITOR must be paid in full before any others.

absorption an accounting procedure employed in ABSORPTION COSTING in which the indirect costs or OVERHEADS of a firm are assigned to production by means of ABSORPTION RATES.

absorption costing a system of product costing that assigns OVERHEAD COSTS in a firm to production by employing a process known as ABSORPTION. The costs are first assigned to cost centers where they are duly absorbed employing ABSORPTION RATES.

absorption rate a rate established for the charging of OVERHEADS to products. The rate that relates budgeted overheads to budgeted cost is calculated in various ways to obtain an overhead rate per unit of product.

abstract of title a document listing the history of a piece of land, such as past claims, MORTGAGES and law suits that may affect the property.

accelerated depreciation a rate of DEPRECIATION that is faster than the rate that is usually allowed for in considering the useful life of an ASSET. This, for example, often happens in the case of high-technology assets where new inventions and innovations are likely to render the assets obsolescent when they are quite new. Accelerated depreciation of an asset is often allowed for in accounts by charging a higher proportion of the cost of the asset to the early years of its life.

acceptance 1 the signature on a BILL OF EXCHANGE that shows that the person on whom the bill is drawn accepts its conditions. **2** a bill of exchange that has been duly accepted in this way.

3 an agreement to accept the terms of an offer.

acceptance sampling a QUALITY-CONTROL process in which a sample is taken from a batch of RAW MATERIALS, WORK IN PROGRESS or finished products and deemed to be representative of the quality of the whole, the whole batch being accepted or rejected on the basis of the sampling.

accepting house a financial institution that specializes in accepting, or guaranteeing to honor, BILLS OF EXCHANGE. By accepting the bills, the accepting house makes the bill more negotiable on the MONEY MARKET and enables the bills to be discounted at more favorable interest rates. Many accepting houses also function as MERCHANT BANKS, especially as there has been a decline in bills of exchange.

acceptor the person who signs the face of a BILL OF EXCHANGE and thereby accepts LIABILITY for it.

accommodation bill a BILL OF EXCHANGE that is signed by the person who is acting as GUARANTOR, such a person being known as the **accommodation party**. If the ACCEPTOR fails to honor the bill on its maturity, the accommodation party is liable for the debt.

accommodation endorsement the endorsement (signing) of a note or draft by a second party to encourage a financial organization, such as a bank or SAVINGS AND LOAN ASSOCIATION, to lend money to a first party whose credit alone would not be sufficient to allow the bank to offer him or her the LOAN. The endorser does not expect to pay the loan in full, but is legally liable to do so if the borrower DEFAULTS.

account 1 a LEDGER record in which is entered all financial transactions that relate to an individual supplier or customer. **2** a statement that records the indebtedness of one person or company to another, often called an INVOICE or bill. **3** the record of the financial dealings between a bank and a bank, such as the depositing of money and the withdrawal of money. **4** a client of an advertising or public-relations agency who pays a fee or commission in return for the services of the agency. **5** a CURRENT ACCOUNT.

accounting the process of recording a company's financial transactions by means of recognized BOOK-KEEPING records and of summarizing these in the form of financial reports, using recognized conventional methods.

accounting earnings the NET INCOME of an organization as shown on its INCOME STATEMENT.

accounting insolvency where a company's total LIABILITIES are greater than its total ASSETS. The company is then unable to meet its DEBTS and is said to be insolvent on the books. See INSOLVENCY.

accounting liquidity indicates how quickly a company's ASSETS could be converted into cash.

accounting period the period over which a company prepares its accounts or financial records. For external purposes, the accounting period is usually a year and LIMITED COMPANIES are required to prepare annual accounts for their shareholders. Internal accounting periods for the purpose of giving managers feedback can be much shorter, such as a month or a quarter.

account payee only words written or printed between two vertical lines drawn across the face of a CHECK. Doing this makes the check non-transferable to try to avoid it being endorsed and paid into a CURRENT ACCOUNT other than that of the payee.

accounts the financial statements of a company prepared from a system of recorded financial transactions. They consist at least of a PROFIT AND LOSS ACCOUNT and the BALANCE SHEET of the company.

accounts payable the money owed by a company to another company or to an individual.

accounts receivable the money that is owed to a company in respect of INVOICES issued.

accrual an expense that is outstanding at the end of an ACCOUNTING PERIOD and requires to be included in the accounts for the period. This often takes the form of a LIABILITY that is not accounted for by an INVOICE or a request for a payment.

accrual accounting an ACCOUNTING procedure in which all the costs and revenue occurring in the course of a company's transactions are counted in the company's accounts on the date on which the costs are incurred or the revenues earned, and not postponed until the costs are actually paid or the revenues actually received.

accumulated profits the amount of PROFIT in a company's ACCOUNTING PERIOD that can be carried forward to the next accounting period after dividends and taxes are paid.

accumulating shares ORDINARY SHARES that are issued to shareholders in a company instead of a DIVIDEND.

active describes a period of lively trading in the STOCK MARKET.

activity-based costing a system of product costing that considers the total cost to the business of making a product and thus aims to break down the division between fixed costs and VARIABLE COSTS. All the costs are related to cost drivers, the various factors that affect the cost of a product.

active box the actual location where SECURITIES are held in a BROKERAGE.

act of God an event caused by natural forces that cannot be predicted. Floods and lightning are acts of God.

actuals COMMODITIES that can be bought and used rather than goods that are traded on the basis of a FUTURES contract.

actuary a trained statistician, often one who is employed by an insurance company to advise on risks and premiums.

administered price a price for a product that is established and controlled by an individual supplier, a group of suppliers or the government rather than being the result of MARKET FORCES.

ad valorem (Latin) "according to value." Referring to a tax that is calculated as a percentage of the total invoice value or price of goods rather than on the number of items involved.

advertising objective a specific target aimed at by advertising, such as increasing the consumer's awareness of a product or brand or improving a company's market share of sales of a product.

advice note a note that is sent to a customer by a supplier to advise him or her that an order for goods has been fulfilled. The advice note is sometimes sent with the goods and sometimes sent separately.

Advisory, Conciliation and Arbitration Service (often abbreviated to **ACAS**) **(Brit)** a UK government-financed body, set up in 1975, that is used to help resolve INDUSTRIAL DISPUTES. The service is used to encourage conciliation and bring the parties in the dispute together and to recommend ARBITRATION services where these are considered appropriate.

affidavit a sworn written statement signed in the presence of an officer, such as a notary public, who is legally empowered to administer oaths.

afghani the standard monetary unit of Afghanistan, made up of 100 PULS.

after the bell after the STOCK MARKET has closed. In the NEW YORK STOCK EXCHANGE a bell is rung to indicate the end of the trading day.

age analysis a summary analysis of how long DEBTS on a company's books have been outstanding, classifying them by the number of months for which they have been outstanding.

agency cross in the STOCK MARKET, a transaction that has a single agent acting for both buyer and seller.

agenda the list of items that have been tabled for discussion at a business meeting, such as a directors' meeting or an ANNUAL GENERAL MEETING.

agent a person appointed by someone, called the PRINCIPAL, to act on his or her behalf in some capacity. An agent, for example, will negotiate between the principal and a third party or act as an intermediary in bringing together buyers and sellers of a commodity or service.

AGM *see* ANNUAL GENERAL MEETING.

agorot *see* SHEQUEL.

agreed bid a TAKEOVER BID that has the backing of the majority of the shareholders of the TARGET COMPANY.

aggressive accounting a method of hiding or disguising losses on INCOME statements in order to satisfy investors and increase STOCK prices.

AIBD Association of International Bond Dealers.

air pocket stock a STOCK MARKET expression for a STOCK where the price has fallen suddenly and dramatically, caused often by unexpected bad news. A reference to the sudden drop in height experienced by passengers on an airplane when it hits an air pocket.

allocation 1 in a company, the breakdown of costs and revenues between different departments or products. **2** the assigning of materials that are held in stock to fulfill product orders.

allotted shares SHARES, previously unissued, that are allocated to intending shareholders who have made application to the company for shares.

allowance 1 money that is paid by an employer to an employee for expenses incurred in the course of his or her work for the company. **3** an agreed time added to the basic time that a worker should take to perform a task, the basic time plus the allowed time to calculate the STANDARD TIME for the task. This allowance makes provision for workers' rest breaks, visits to the bathroom, etc. **4** the additional raw materials or component parts that are added to the basic materials allowed for the completion of a particular product. This allowance allows for such things as anticipated wastage. **5** a price reduction or rebate that is given to a customer for some reason, such as an exceptionally large order.

allowance for bad debt an amount a company is owed for goods supplied on CREDIT, but which is unlikely to be paid by the DEBTOR.

amalgamation the combination of two or more companies. The amalgamation may come about by the merging of two or more existing companies, by one company acquiring other companies or by one new company being formed from existing companies that have been dissolved. See also MERGER, TAKEOVER BID.

American Bankers Association (ABA) founded in 1875, the ABA keeps its members informed of up-to-date banking procedures, upholds standards of banking management and service and develops educational opportunities for banking personnel.

American Bar Association (ABA) founded in 1878, this is an association of practitioners in law at every level. It endeavors to improve legal education and uphold standards.

American Depositary Receipt (ADR) a receipt issued by a US depositary bank representing foreign SHARES held by the bank.

American Federation of Labor – Congress of Industrial Organizations (AFL-CIO) the largest labor union in the US, formed by the merger of the two most powerful unions in 1955.

American Management Association (AMA) a professional organization, founded in 1923, which promotes training and information services to managers.

American Marketing Association (AMA) a professional organization that promotes good practice in the field of sales and marketing.

American National Standards Institute (ANSI) an association of industrial companics, tradc associations, consumer and technical organizations and government agencies that establishes best practice standards for most industries.

American Stock Exchange (AMEX) thc sccond largest STOCK EXCHANGE in the USA.

amortization 1 the repayment of debt by a borrower in a series of installments, made up of part interest, part capital repayment over a period of time. **2** the system of regarding as an expense the annual amount that is considered to waste away from a FIXED ASSET, such as a LEASE.

analyst in finance, person who works for a BRO-

KERAGE or other financial institution, studying the performance of companies and makes buy or sell recommendations to his or her clients.

angel a person who provides VENTURE CAPITAL for a new business.

annual accounts the financial statements of a company or organization that are published annually. The accounts consist of the PROFIT AND LOSS ACCOUNT, the BALANCE SHEET, the statement of total recognized gains and losses, the director's report and the AUDITORS' report.

annual general meeting (abbreviation **AGM**) an annual meeting of the shareholders of a company that by law must be called to allow the shareholders an opportunity to discuss the ANNUAL ACCOUNTS. The shareholders at the meeting also are involved in the recommendations for DIVIDENDS and the appointment of directors and AUDITORS.

annual percentage rate (often abbreviated to **APR**) an INTEREST RATE expressed as the rate for the year. For example, credit card companies are required to quote an annual percentage rate to potential customers.

annual report the annual record of a public company's financial situation.

annual return (Brit) a document that by law must be filed with the REGISTRAR OF COMPANIES within fourteen days of the occurrence of the ANNUAL

GENERAL MEETING. The information given on the document includes the address of the registered office of the company, the names, addresses, nationalities and occupations of its directors. Attached to the annual return must be the company's financial statements, the directors' report and the auditor's report. Small-sized companies and medium-sized companies may be allowed to file an abbreviated form of accounts.

annuity 1 a contract between an individual and an insurance company in which the individual pays a premium to the company, usually in the form of a lump sum of money, and the company in return pays him or her an agreed sum of money at regular, periodic intervals for the rest of his or her life or for an agreed, specified length of time. **2** the payment made on the basis of such a contract.

anonymous trading transactions made on the STOCK MARKET without the names of either buyer or seller being revealed.

antedate to date a document, such as a check, before the date on which it was drawn up.

antitrust laws laws designed to prevent the formation of monopolies and stop trade restrictions such as price-fixing. The Sherman Antitrust Act (1890) was one of the first such laws, outlawing monopoly and promoting free competition. *See also* CLAYTON ACT.

application for listing the process by which a company makes an application to a STOCK EXCHANGE so that its securities can be traded on it. This enables the company to raise CAPITAL by issuing SHARES on the stock exchange.

appreciation 1 an increase in the value of an ASSET such as land or a building, usually as a result of INFLATION. *See* DEPRECIATION. **2** an increase in the value of one foreign currency against another or others in a floating exchange system.

appropriation 1 an allocation of the NET PROFITS of a company in its accounts. **2** the allocation of payments to one particular DEBT of several debts owed by the same debtor.

approved deferred share trust a TRUST FUND set up by a company that purchases SHARES in the company for the benefit of its employees, tax on any DIVIDENDS being deferred until the shares have been sold and then paid at a reduced rate.

APR the abbreviated form of ANNUAL PERCENTAGE RATE.

arbitrage the buying and selling of COMMODITIES, financial securities or foreign currencies between two or more markets so as to be able to take advantage of any differences in prices, interest rates or exchange rates.

arbitration a procedure for settling an INDUSTRIAL DISPUTE in which a third party is called in to settle the dispute and make an award or come to a conclusion that is binding on the two conflicting parties.

ARMs adjustable rate mortgages.

arm's length (of a price or transaction) indicating that both buyer and seller are free agents, there is no conflict of interest and both parties willingly agree to the price or transaction.

arrears a DEBT that has not been settled by the due date.

articles of association the legal constitution of a company that sets out the rights and duties of the company's shareholders and also sets out the powers of management, the running of directors' meetings and shareholders' meetings.

A-shares ORDINARY SHARES in a company that usually do not confer voting rights on their owners.

Asian currency units (ACUs) dollar deposits held in Asian locations, such as Singapore.

ask price the lowest price a DEALER will accept for STOCK he or she wishes to sell.

asset an article or property that is owned by a company or individual and has a monetary value. *See* FIXED ASSET, CURRENT ASSET, DEPRECIATION, ACCELERATED DEPRECIATION.

asset classes the various groups of ASSETS such as BONDS, SHARES, foreign investments and REAL ESTATE.

asset-stripping the acquisition of a company by

another company or individual with a view to selling the ASSETS of the TARGET COMPANY for financial profit rather than with a view to running it as a GOING CONCERN.

asset turnover the proportion of NET sales to total ASSETS.

asset value per share the total value of the ASSETS of a company minus its LIABILITIES divided by the number of ORDINARY SHARES. This represents the theoretical value of the amount each share would be worth if the company was wound up, although the real value is likely to be less.

assimilation in the STOCK MARKET, the absorption of a NEW ISSUE of STOCK by the public.

associated company a company in which another company has a significant interest but not a majority interest.

at *see* KIP.

auction market markets where products are bought and sold through free interplay between buyers and sellers. The STOCK EXCHANGES are auction markets.

audit an independent examination of a company's financial statements by a qualified AUDITOR so that he or she can give an expert opinion as to whether the financial statements give an accurate and fair picture of the financial state of affairs of the company.

auditor a professional accountant who is trained

to conduct an independent assessment of the accuracy and fairness of a company's financial statements, called an AUDIT.

auditor's report the section of an ANNUAL REPORT in which the AUDITOR comments on the company's financial statements.

authorized share capital the maximum amount of share capital that may be issued by a company as set out in the company's ARTICLES OF ASSOCIATION.

automated clearing houses (ACH) the 32 regional interbank networks which undertake electronic transactions.

automatic teller machine (ATM) a machine that can undertake simple banking transactions, such as deposits and withdrawals, without the customer having to go into the bank itself.

autoregressive using information from past events to predict future events.

availability float checks payable to a company but which have not yet been cleared.

average in the STOCK MARKET, a selection of STOCKS whose performance is intended to represent the movement of the market in general. For example, the Dow Jones Industrial Average.

average cost the unit cost of a product estimated by dividing the total output cost by the total number of units produced.

average stock a method of accounting for stock

movements that assumes that goods are taken out of stock at the average cost of the goods in stock.

avo the monetary unit of Macao, equal to one hundredth of a PATACA.

B

baby boomer a colloquial expression used to describe a person born between 1946 and 1962. Baby boomers are considered to be commercially astute and demanding consumers.

backdate to put an earlier date on a document or a check than that on which it was drawn up, making the document or check effective from the earlier date.

back office where the clerical work, accounting and record-keeping is undertaken in banking and other financial institutions.

back-to-back loan a loan arrangement in which money is lent by a company in one country to a company in another, usually in a different currency.

back up the truck a STOCK MARKET expression for when a large purchaser buys up significant amounts of a single STOCK.

backwardation the difference between the SPOT PRICE of a commodity and the FORWARD PRICE.

bad debt an amount of money owed that is considered unlikely ever to be repaid.

baht the monetary unit of Thailand, made up of 100 SATANG.

baiza the monetary unit of Oman, equal to one hundredth of a RIAL.

balance of payments the record of a country's trading deals and financial transactions with other countries in the world.

balance of trade the record of a country's trading deals with other countries in the world. It is a component part of the BALANCE OF PAYMENTS.

balance sheet an accounting statement of the assets, both FIXED ASSETS and CURRENT ASSETS, and LIABILITIES of a company issued on the last day of an ACCOUNTING PERIOD or trading period.

balboa *see* CENTESIMO.

balloon mortgage a MORTGAGE in which at the end of the mortgage agreement period there is still some of the original CAPITAL and some INTEREST outstanding. At the end of the mortgage period a lump sum has to be paid to settle the outstanding debt.

bank bill a BILL OF EXCHANGE that is issued or guaranteed (accepted) by a bank.

bank charge the amount that a bank charges a customer for a specific transaction.

bank collection float the time taken between the depositing of a check and the funds from that check being available.

bank deposit an amount of money that a customer places in a bank account for safekeeping or for earning INTEREST.

bank draft a check that is drawn by a bank on itself or on one of its agents. Bank drafts are usually used in situations in which the person who is going to receive the money is unwilling to accept a check. A draft, unlike a check, carries no risk of not being honored. In the case of a bank draft the person who wishes to make a payment buys the draft from the bank.

banker's acceptance (Brit) a form of PROMISSORY NOTE that promises to pay a certain sum of money and has been accepted by a bank.

bank examiner the representative of a Federal or state agency who AUDITS the financial and managerial performance of banks.

Bank for International Settlements (BIS) an international bank based in Basel, Switzerland, that monitors banking activity worldwide and establishes rules governing bank regulation.

bank loan a specified sum of money that has been lent to an individual or company (the borrower) by a bank, usually for a fixed period of time and usually at a specified rate of INTEREST. In cases where there is considered to be a degree of risk attached to the loan, the bank calls for some form of security to act as COLLATERAL for the loan. Thus bank loans may be secured or unsecured. *See* SECURED LOAN, UNSECURED LOAN.

bank note a note which is issued for general use as money. It carries no interest. In the USA, the Federal Reserve Bank is the only bank that can issue a bank note.

bank rate the rate at which the central bank, in the case of the USA the FEDERAL RESERVE BANK, makes loans to member banks.

bank reconciliation statement a statement showing how the bank balance of a company can be reconciled with the BANK STATEMENT. The bank reconciliation statement shows which entries make up the difference between the two, the difference occurring, for example, because of checks that have been drawn but not yet presented or checks paid in to the bank but not yet credited to the company and bank charges that have been deducted by the bank from the company's account but not yet recorded by the company in its records. Bank reconciliation statements are performed on a regular basis as an in-company control check.

bank run a panic situation where depositors, afraid that the bank will collapse, rush to withdraw their money from it.

bankruptcy the state of individuals who are unable to pay their debts and who seem to have no reasonable prospects of so doing, and against whom a court **bankruptcy order** has been issued. This order deprives the bankrupt party of his or her property so that this can be used to pay off creditors as far as possible. Some property, such as equipment that is required for his or her business or employment, essential domestic equipment, is exempted.

bankruptcy risk the possibility that an organization will not be able to settle its DEBTS.

bank statement a statement issued regularly by a bank or building society that records the financial transactions of an individual or company. It shows the credit and debit entries and the current balance.

bank wire computerized system linking the major banks and used only for transferring information, not for payments.

bar (slang) one million dollars.

barbell strategy *see* DUMBBELL.

bar chart a diagram that indicates statistical data, such as sales figures, by means of bars or rectangles of varying heights.

bar code a code in the form of a series of lines and spaces that is printed on the packaging of products for sale in retail shops. This is 'read' at the checkout point by a laser scanner and the price and description of goods displayed on the till, the stock record being automatically reduced at the same time.

base rate the hourly rate for a specific job, not including overtime pay or shift differential.

base stock a volume of stock held by a company that is assumed to be at a constant level, stock levels not being allowed to fall below this level. When valuation of stock takes place, this volume of stock is valued at its original cost.

basket of currencies a group of selected currencies that is used to set a value on some other currency.

batch costing a form of product costing in which UNIT COSTS are given on the basis of a batch produced. *See* BATCH PRODUCTION.

batch production a form of manufacturing production in which a number of identical products or components are passed through the various production processes as a batch.

batch size the number of items that make up a batch in BATCH PRODUCTION.

bear a dealer on a STOCK EXCHANGE or currency market who operates on the expectation that prices are going to fall. *See* BULL.

bearer bond a BOND whose owner's name is not listed on the issuing company's books and is payable to the holder. It does not need to be endorsed.

bearer instrument a BOND or CHECK that does not show the payee's name. It can, therefore, be cashed by anyone and, like a BEARER BOND, does not need to be endorsed.

bearish *see* BULLISH.

bear market a situation on the STOCK EXCHANGE or currency market in which there is persistent selling and limited buying, thereby causing prices to fall.

bear raid in the STOCK MARKET, when large traders sell STOCKS with the intention of forcing prices down.

bed and breakfast (Brit) a process on the STOCK EXCHANGE in which a shareholder sells SHARES at the end of a trading day and buys them back when trading opens the next morning. This process is carried out in connection with CAPITAL GAINS TAX, the object being to establish a loss.

beggar-thy-neighbor an international trade policy that uses means such as protective barriers to increase one country's competitiveness against other countries.

below-the-line 1 referring to entries that occur below the horizontal line in a company's PROFIT AND LOSS ACCOUNT. *See* ABOVE-THE-LINE. **2** referring to expenditure on advertising that does not involve payments of commission or fees to an advertising agency. Such advertising expenditure relates, for example, to POINT-OF-SALE advertising, direct-mail advertising, and so on.

benchmarking the process undergone by a company of trying to establish the best production and marketing practices with a view to using this as a guide or benchmark to methods to improve the efficiency of its own production and marketing techniques.

benefits in kind benefits other than actual cash that

a person obtains from his or her employment. Such benefits include company cars, private medical insurance and low-interest loans.

bid price the price at which a dealer in a FINANCIAL SECURITY, foreign currency or COMMODITY is prepared to buy.

bid-asked spread the difference between the BID and the ASK prices.

bidder a company or person who wishes to buy a firm or a SECURITY.

Big Bang the informal name given to the occurrence of major changes on the London Stock Exchange which were introduced on October 27 1986.

Big Board popular name for the NEW YORK STOCK EXCHANGE listings of STOCK prices.

Big Uglies in the STOCK MARKET, the popular name for traditional industries such as mining and steel manufacturing.

bill *see* ACCOUNT 1.

bill broker a broker who buys BILLS OF EXCHANGE from traders and sells them to banks or DISCOUNT HOUSES, or, alternatively, holds them until the date of their maturity.

bill of exchange a written order instructing one person to pay a certain sum of money to a named person on demand or at a specified time in the future.

bill of lading a CONTRACT between an exporter and

a carrier which specifies the conditions under which the goods are to be delivered to the recipient.

bill of sale a document by which a person transfers to another the ownership of goods.

bill of specific performance a legal document that compels a party to a CONTRACT to fulfill the conditions of the contract exactly as specified.

bill rate the rate at which BILLS OF EXCHANGE are discounted by banks, DISCOUNT HOUSES, etc.

birr the standard monetary unit of Ethiopia and Eritrea, made up of 100 cents.

black economy a form of economic activity that is undisclosed, unrecorded and thus not liable for taxation. In some cases people involved not only evade tax payments but are also illegally working when they are in receipt of state benefits.

black knight an individual or company that makes an unwelcome or hostile TAKEOVER BID for a company. *See* GRAY KNIGHT, WHITE KNIGHT, YELLOW KNIGHT.

blacklist a hypothetical list that identifies people or organizations that are to be avoided for various reasons, such as inability to pay DEBTS, political sympathies and so on.

black market an illegal market for a commodity or service, either because these are rationed by government, as in wartime, or forbidden, as with drugs.

Black Tuesday refers to 29 October, 1929, the day of the great STOCK MARKET CRASH.

Blitzkrieg tender offer (German: Blitz = lightning; Krieg = war) a TAKEOVER BID that is intended to be irresistible, so that the takeover will proceed quickly and without problems. *See also* GODFATHER OFFER.

blocked account 1 a bank account from which money may not be withdrawn, even when this is not overdrawn. One of a number of reasons for this is that the holder of the account is undergoing BANKRUPTCY or INSOLVENCY proceedings. **2** a bank account in the name of an exporter of goods in another country into which money from a sale of goods has been paid but from which the money cannot be transferred to the country in which the exporter resides. This situation can occur, for example, when a government is short of foreign currency.

blocked currency a currency that, because of strict exchange controls, cannot be removed from a country and is not freely convertible into other currencies.

block house a BROKERAGE that finds clients to buy or sell large amounts of STOCKS. *See* BLOCK TRADE.

block trade trading in very large amounts of SHARES in the same company, usually sold as a single unit and with, for example, a market value of $200,000 or higher.

block voting where SHAREHOLDERS agree to combine their SHARES in a single block, so as to increase their voting power.

blow-off top in the STOCK MARKET, a situation where SHARE prices rise sharply then fall equally sharply.

blue-chip company a company with considerable ASSETS and a well-established reputation so that its SHARES are considered to be a particularly low-risk investment. American in origin, the term takes its name from the color of the highest value chip used in the game of poker.

blue-collar worker a manual worker, so called because of the blue overalls worn by manual workers in factories, etc. *See* WHITE-COLLAR WORKER.

blue-sky laws state laws intended to protect the public from fraudulent investment deals.

board of directors a group of DIRECTORS responsible for running a company.

bogey 1 an output standard that worker sets for himself or herself. **2.** in investing, the RETURN an INVESTMENT MANAGER is set against to evaluate his or her performance.

boilerplate standard terms and conditions found on contracts and other legal documents.

bolivar the standard monetary unit of Venezuela, made up of 100 CENTIMOS.

boliviano the standard monetary unit of Bolivia, made up of 100 CENTAVOS.

bond a FINANCIAL SECURITY that is issued by a borrower, such as a company, a local authority or the government, to a lender, such as an individual, a commercial bank or an institution. Bonds are usually issued for a set number of years and are generally fixed-interest. Once issued, bonds can be bought and sold on the STOCK MARKET.

bonded goods goods on which CUSTOMS DUTY has not yet been paid, although the goods are liable for duty.

bonded warehouse a warehouse for the storing of goods that are liable for duty but on which CUSTOMS DUTY has not yet been paid. *See* BONDED GOODS.

bonus 1 an extra payment made to employees as an incentive payment for achieving high productivity levels, exceptionally high sales figures or as a share of the profits of a particularly good year's trading. The payment is usually paid in cash but it can take the form of shares in the company. **2** an extra amount of money that is paid by an insurer to a policy holder in addition to the money payable on a LIFE-INSURANCE policy.

bonus dividend a DIVIDEND that is issued to SHAREHOLDERS of a company in addition to those that are expected.

bonus payment *see* BONUS 1.

bonus shares additional SHARES that are issued to existing SHAREHOLDERS in a company without any further payment being made by them.

book-keeping the keeping of the account books of a company. *See* ACCOUNTING.

book value the value of an ASSET as it is stated in the account books of a company.

boom a period of economic activity, full-capacity levels of production, high levels of employment, high demand, high wages and high prices. This can lead to an excessive level of INFLATION and, if not tightly controlled, to a RECESSION and perhaps even a SLUMP.

borrow to obtain money as a LOAN and with the understanding that it is to be repaid, usually with INTEREST.

bottom fisher in the STOCK MARKET, an investor who looks for possibilities in STOCKS whose prices have fallen but which may, in fact, be undervalued.

bottom line a term used in accounting to denote the NET PROFIT from a business after all costs have been paid.

bought deal a method of raising CAPITAL used by a company in which MARKET MAKERS or banks are invited to bid for new SHARES, these then being sold to the highest bidder who then sells them on the STOCK MARKET with a view to making a profit.

bounce a check writing a check on a depository account knowing that there is not enough money in the account for the check to clear.

Bourse (French) a term used in Europe to refer generally to a STOCK MARKET. The Paris Bourse is the main French stock market.

brand a particular product that is produced or distributed by a company, distinguished from products offered by competing companies by a name, symbol or design. A brand may be given legal protection through the use of TRADE-MARK or COPYRIGHT.

brand extension the use of an existing successful BRAND NAME to launch a new or modified product, sometimes in a different category of merchandise, the hope being that the popularity enjoyed by the original product will spread to the new or modified product.

brand image the perception of BRAND that manufacturers and distributors try to create in consumers by advertising, SALES PROMOTION, etc, in order to persuade them to buy it and to keep buying it.

brand loyalty the tendency shown by consumers to buy a particular brand and to keep on buying it. This is partly owing to satisfaction with the product and partly a result of successful advertising and SALES PROMOTION.

brand mark the symbol, distinctive lettering or design that is used to indicate a particular BRAND of product.

brand name the name that is used to identify a particular product, manufacturer or distributor.

brand value the value that is attached to a BRAND NAME. This can be an important INTANGIBLE ASSET to a company, for example in a TAKEOVER BID situation.

breach of contract a failure of one of the parties involved in a contract to carry out the obligations imposed by the contract.

break in the STOCK MARKET, a sudden, sharp fall in prices.

breakeven point the level of production, sales, etc, at which a company makes neither a profit nor loss.

breaking bulk the practice of intermediaries in a DISTRIBUTION CHANNEL of buying large quantities (BULK BUYING) of goods and then selling on smaller quantities of these to customers.

break-up value the value of an ASSET of a company as estimated if it was sold off separately as opposed to being sold as part of the sale of a company as a GOING CONCERN.

bridge loan a form of short-term LOAN taken out by a borrower to bridge the gap between the purchase of one ASSET and the sale of another, such as the purchase of one house and the sale of another.

British clearers (Brit) *see* CLEARING BANK.

British Standards Institution (Brit) (often abbreviated to **BSI**) an organization the function of which is to establish and formulate national standards of quality for products and processes in certain industries, such as engineering, electrical engineering, building, etc, the products that meet the requisite standard being entitled to show this by the use of a 'kitemark' logo.

broker an agent or intermediary who brings together two sides of a contract, such as a buyer and a seller of financial ASSETS.

brokerage 1 the business of a BROKER **2** fee charged by a BROKER.

brokerage house an investment securities firm.

broker's loan a LOAN made by a bank to a stockbroker and secured by STOCK.

BSI (Brit) the abbreviated form of BRITISH STANDARDS INSTITUTION.

bubble in the STOCK MARKET, a volatile period where SHARE values rise and then fall sharply. The dotcom bubble of the 1990s is an example.

buck STOCK MARKET slang for one million dollars.

bucket shop colloquial expression for BROKERAGE firms that, amongst other fraudulent practices, use aggressive telephone sales techniques to arrange deals in worthless or non-existent SECURITIES.

buck the trend STOCK MARKET slang for a STOCK whose price is rising or falling in the opposite direction to prices in the market in general.

budget a financial statement containing a company's plans and policies for a specified ACCOUNTING PERIOD.

budget deficit the amount by which spending exceeds INCOME. Used particularly to refer to government performance.

building society (Brit) a financial institution that accepts deposits from savers and makes long-term loans for house purchase secured by MORTGAGE.

bulk-buying the purchase of products, commodities, etc, in large quantities, often in order to obtain a discount on the usual price.

bull a dealer on a STOCK EXCHANGE or currency market who operates on the expectation that prices will rise.

bulldog bond (Brit) a BOND issued in London.

bulldog market (Brit) the investment market in the UK.

bullet contract a guaranteed investment bought with a single PREMIUM.

bullion precious metals, such as gold, silver, platinum, etc, that are used in the form of bars or ingots.

bullish, bearish in the STOCK MARKET, describing the prevailing attitudes of investors. Bullish indicates an optimistic outlook, while bearish indicates a pessimistic outlook. *See* also BULL, BEAR.

bull market a situation on the STOCK EXCHANGE or currency market in which there is persistent buying and limited selling, thereby causing prices to rise.

burn rate in finance, a term describing the rate at which a new organization uses its CAPITAL to pay for its business activities, before it can do so from INCOME from those activities.

business cycle the process by which business and economic activity tends to fluctuate up and down in a relatively regular pattern.

business failure business that has closed while still owing money to its CREDITORS.

business plan a detailed statement of the aims and plans of a business over a stated period.

butut *see* DALASI.

buy back where a company buys back its SHARES on the STOCK MARKET, possibly to increase the value of the shares still available.

buying on margin where investors in the STOCK MARKET borrow money to buy STOCKS, gambling on the SHARE value rising enough to allow them to pay the money back and make a PROFIT.

buy-out *see* MANAGEMENT BUY-OUT.

C

calendar in the STOCK MARKET, the list of NEW IS-SUES that are about to become available.

calendar effect a term describing the way STOCKS tend to perform differently at different times, influenced by such events as the day of the week, holidays and the month of the year.

calendar year the calendar year runs from January 1 to December 31. *See also* FISCAL YEAR.

callable bonds fixed rate bonds the issuer of which has the right to redeem or call the bond at par during the bond's' lifetime.

call report a report that is completed at regular intervals by a sales representative indicating the number of sales calls made and the results of these, such as the number of sales concluded.

Canadian agencies Canadian agency banks established in the USA.

cancelled check a CHECK paid and charged to an account and stamped with the name of the drawee bank and the date of the transaction. A cancelled check proves that something was paid for and the date it was paid.

capital 1 the funds that are invested in a business consisting either of SHARE CAPITAL, provided by the shares of share-holders or LOAN CAPITAL, provided by lenders by way of loans. **2** the total value of the assets that a person holds minus any liabilities. **3** plant or machinery that is used by a company in the production of goods or services.

capital allocation decision the separation of funds in an investment PORTFOLIO into RISK-FREE and more uncertain ventures.

capital asset an asset that is expected to be used long-term in a business. Capital assets include buildings, plant and machinery. *See also* FIXED ASSET.

capital budgeting the process of planning future expenditure in a firm.

capital expenditure the expenditure by a company on the purchase or improvement of a fixed or CAPITAL ASSET. This expenditure is not charged against the profits of the company when the expenditure takes place but is written off against profits over several accounting periods. See also FIXED ASSET.

capital gain the financial gain made when an ASSET is realized, the gain being equal to the difference between the cost of the asset and the price that was paid for it on its disposal.

capital gains tax (Brit) a tax that is payable on CAPITAL GAIN. Currently in the UK capital gains of up to £6,300 per year are exempt from the tax. Examples of other exemptions include gains on main dwelling houses, LIFE ASSURANCE and government securities.

capitalism an economic and political system in which individuals are free to dispose of their CAPITAL without major interference from the government.

capitalization 1 the provision of CAPITAL for a company or organization. **2** the structure of the capital of a company or organization, indicating the extent to which capital is made up of share capital, whether ORDINARY SHARES or PREFERENCE SHARES, and the extent to which the capital is made up of LOAN CAPITAL. **3** the conversion to capital of the financial reserves of a company by means of a SCRIP ISSUE.

capital loss the deficit that occurs when a capital ASSET realizes a price that is lower than the original cost of the asset.

capital reserves PROFITS that are not distributed to shareholders as DIVIDENDS. Such reserves include profits gained on the revaluation of CAPITAL ASSETS and any sums of money that are obtained from share issues in excess of the nominal value of the SHARES.

capital structure 1 the composition of the CAPITAL of a company or organization indicating the portion of capital that is made up of shares and the portion that is made up of LOAN CAPITAL, having been borrowed either in the long-term or in the short-term. **2** the balance between the ASSETS and LIABILITIES of a company.

capital turnover the ratio of sales to the CAPITAL employed in a company.

captive market a group of people who are in such a position for some reason or other that they are obliged to buy a particular product or products instead of having access to a range of goods in which they have an element of choice.

captive product a product that has to be purchased on a continuing basis because it has to be used with another main product, for example razor blades for a razor.

captive product pricing the pricing of a CAPTIVE PRODUCT.

career break an interruption to the career of in- dividual, usually for the purpose of taking care of children but sometimes for other reasons, such as further education or the achievement of some personal goal, such as travel.

carload rate in transportation, the rate that applies to a shipment of goods on the railroad that oc- cupies a complete railroad car rather than just a section of it. Carload rates are the best rates available for railroad shipment.

carrier a person or firm that transports goods or people from place to place for a fee.

carrier rate the rate charged by a carrier for trans- porting goods. The carrier rate is usually based on units of weight, but it can also be based on the size or bulk of the item to be carried.

carrier's lien the legal right of a transporter to retain goods shipped as collateral for payment for transportation costs. *See also* LIEN, INNKEEPER'S LIEN, MECHANIC'S LIEN.

cartel an association of suppliers formed to regulate prices and sales conditions, either wholly or in part, of the goods or services that they provide. Such cartels can be national or international, although in some countries such as the US and the UK, cartels are forbidden.

cash legal tender in the form of coins and banknotes.

cash cow an expression used to describe a business that generates high PROFITS and a constant, substantial CASH FLOW.

cash deal (Brit) a financial transaction on the London Stock Exchange in which settlement is made right away, usually on the date after the transaction has taken place.

cash discount a reduction in the money owed by a customer to a supplier of goods and services in return for prompt payment or in return for payment in CASH.

cash dividend a dividend that is paid in CASH rather than in shares. Such payments are made NET of tax.

cash flow the money coming into a business from

sales and receipts and going out of the business in the form of payments to suppliers, employees and creditors.

cashier's check a CHECK drawn on the bank's own funds and signed by a cashier or other authorized official.

cash market in the STOCK MARKET, a situation where transactions are completed promptly, with transfer of ownership and payment taking place immediately or very quickly. *See also* SPOT MARKET.

cash on delivery an arrangement by which goods that have been ordered are paid for at the time of delivery.

cashout when a firm has no CASH readily available and no immediate prospect of getting any.

cash ratio the proportion of a company's ASSETS kept as CASH.

cash reserve CASH held by a business that is not required for immediate needs, but available for unexpected contingencies.

casino finance in the STOCK MARKET, a popular expression for a very high-risk investment strategy.

catalog store a retail outlet in which there are very few goods on display, the majority being sold through the medium of a catalog in which the goods are displayed.

category killer in the STOCK MARKET, a reference to

large companies that squeeze smaller competitors out of business.

caveat emptor (Latin) "let the buyer beware." Before making any purchase or investment, the buyer should know his or her rights and take every possible precaution.

CBI (Brit) the abbreviation for CONFEDERATION OF BRITISH INDUSTRY.

cease and desist order an order imposed by the Federal Trade Commission that compels an organization to stop an unfair business practice.

cedi *see* PESEWA.

cent *see* BIRR, DOLLAR, GUILDER, LEONE, LILANGENI, LIRA 3, NEW SOL, POUND, RAND, RUPEE, SHILLING.

centavo 1 a monetary unit of Bolivia, equal to one hundredth of a BOLIVIANO. **2** a monetary unit of Brazil, equal to one hundredth of a cruzeiro. **3** a monetary unit of Argentina, Chile, Colombia, Cuba, the Dominican Republic, Guinea-Bissau, Mexico and the Philippines, equal to one hundredth of a PESO. **4** a monetary unit of Ecuador, equal to one hundredth of a SUCRE. **5** a monetary unit of El Salvador, equal to one hundredth of a COLON. **6** a monetary unit of Guatemala, equal to one hundredth of a QUETZAL. **7** a monetary unit of Honduras, equal to one hundredth of a LEMPIRA. **8** a monetary unit of Nicaragua, equal to one hundredth of a CORDOBA. **9** a monetary unit of Cape Verde and

Madeira, equal to one hundredth of an ESCUDO.
10 a monetary unit of Mozambique, equal to
one hundredth of a metical. **11** a monetary unit
of São Tomé e Principe, equal to one hundredth
of a DOBRA. **12** a former currency of Portgual,
replaced by the Euro on January 1 2002.

centesimo 1 a former monetary unit of Italy and
San Marino, equal to one hundredth of a LIRA,
and replaced by the Euro on January 1 2002. **2**
a monetary unit of Panama, equal to one hundredth of a balboa. **3** a monetary unit of Uruguay, equal to one hundredth of a PESO.

centime 1 a monetary unit of Andorra, Benin,
Burkina-Faso, Burundi, Cameroon, the Central African Republic, Chad, Comoros, the
Congo, Côte d'Ivoire, Djibouti, Equatorial
Guinea, Gabon, Guinea, Liechtenstein, Madagascar, Mali, Monaco, Niger, Rwanda, Senegal, Switzerland, Tahiti and Togo, equal to one
hundredth of a FRANC. **2** a monetary unit of Algeria, equal to one hundredth of a DINAR. **3** a
monetary unit of Haiti, equal to one hundredth
of a gourde. **4** a monetary unit of Morocco,
equal to one hundredth of a DIRHAM. **5** a former
monetary unit of Belgium, France and Luxembourg, now replaced by the Euro on January 1 2002.

centimo 1 a monetary unit of Costa Rica, equal to
one hundredth of a COLON. **2** a monetary unit of

Paragauy, equal to one hundredth of a GUARANI. 3 a former monetary unit of Spain and Andorra, equal to one hundredth of a PESETA replaced by the Euro on January 1 2002. 4 a monetary unit of Venezuela, equal to one hundredth of a BOLIVAR.

central bank the leading bank in a country that provides banking services to the country's government and the commercial banking system and is responsible for implementing monetary policy.

CE(O) the abbreviation for CHIEF EXECUTIVE (OFFICER).

certificate of origin (Brit) a document that states the country from which a consignment of goods has originated in international trading. In the UK and some other countries it is usually a CHAMBER OF COMMERCE that issues such a certificate.

certificates of deposit (CDs) CDs are bought from banks or other financial institutions and are repayable on a fixed date, usually with INTEREST

certified check a personal CHECK for which the issuing bank guarantees that there are sufficient funds in the depositor's account to pay the amount specified when the check is present for payment.

certified public accountant (CPA) a registered accountant who has achieved the necessary standard of competency required by the state. Requirements vary from state to state, but certification from one state is generally acceptable in another state.

certified stock STOCKS of a COMMODITY that have been passed as acceptable in fulfillment of CONTRACTS on a FUTURES market.

CFAT abbreviation for cash flow after taxes.

CFTC abbreviation for the Commodity Futures Trading Commission, a Federal agency that regulates FUTURES trading.

chairman/chairperson the most senior member of management who presides at meetings of the board of directors of a company and at the ANNUAL GENERAL MEETING of the company. The chairman/chairperson may be little more than a figurehead in a company and not play any executive role in the day-to-day running of the company and he/she may have a dual role, especially in a small company, of chairman/chairperson and MANAGING DIRECTOR.

chairman's report a report that gives a summary of the year's activities of a company and a short survey of the likely activities of the coming year. It is usually read aloud by the chairman at the ANNUAL GENERAL MEETING of a company and is often included in the company's ANNUAL REPORT.

chamber of commerce (Brit) an organization that acts as a forum and advice and information center for local business people and traders in a town or city. Chambers of commerce also provide training facilities and are responsible for the issuing of CERTIFICATES OF ORIGIN. In the UK most chambers of commerce are affiliated to the British Chamber of Commerce.

channel of distribution the route along which products move from the manufacturer to the eventual consumer.

channel stuffing an expression used to describe a situation when a company deliberately sends the retailers along their CHANNEL OF DISTRIBUTION more products than they are actually able to sell, thereby increasing the company's ACCOUNTS RECEIVABLE, or money owed. This is usually done to raise the value of a company's STOCK. Channel stuffing rebounds on the company when the retailers return all the unsold goods. Channel stuffing is illegal.

charitable trust (Brit) a trust that is set up for some charitable purpose and that is registered with the CHARITY COMMISSIONERS. Charitable trusts do not have to pay INCOME TAX if they satisfy the regulations set out by the CHARITY COMMISSIONERS.

Charity Commissioners (Brit) the board that advises, investigates and registers charities. It is governed by the Charities Act of 1993 and is responsible to parliament.

chartism the use of charts, diagrams and graphs to monitor price movements of shares, foreign currencies, etc, with a view to trying to forecast future price movements.

check a preprinted form on which instructions are given to an account holder, such as a bank, to pay a stated sum to a named recipient.

checking account a bank account on which checks can be drawn.

cherry picking in the STOCK MARKET, when investors choose only investments that have already performed well in the hope that the upward trend will continue.

chetrum a monetary unit of Bhutan, equal to one hundredth of a ngultrum.

Chicago Mercantile Exchange (CME) an organization that disseminates market information, enforces trading rules and provides a location for trading.

chief executive (officer) (Brit) (often abbreviated to **CE** or **CEO**) the person in a company or organization who has overall responsibility for the management of a firm, often now used in the UK instead of the term MANAGING DIRECTOR.

Chinese wall the segregation of the various sections of a financial institution or business so as to prevent information spreading from one section to another with a view to protecting the interests of the clients. For example, the market-making section of a firm would be segregated in this way from the broking section so that advice to clients will be impartial.

chon a monetary unit of North Korea and South Korea, equal to one hundredth of a won.

churning over-trading of a client's account, usually to increase the BROKER'S COMMISSION, rather than the client's wealth.

circuit breaker in the STOCK MARKET, measures which are taken to avert panic selling. Such measures may include stopping all trading for one hour.

circulating capital *same as* WORKING CAPITAL.

City (Brit) the part of London in which are situated the head offices of many financial institutions and which is located on the square mile on the north side of the River Thames between Waterloo Bridge and Tower Bridge. In recent times some of the financial institutions have begun to migrate from this area, for example, to the Docklands area.

Clayton Act an American ANTITRUST LAW, passed in 1914, which prohibits price discrimination.

clawback money that a government retrieves from people who have been given some form of benefit, the money being 'clawed back' in the form of taxes.

clean opinion an AUDITOR's statement which indicates his or her unreserved acceptance of an organization's financial statements.

clean price the price of a GILT-EDGED SECURITY excluding the interest that has accrued since payment of the previous DIVIDEND.

clearing bank (Brit) a bank in the UK that is a member of the bankers' CLEARING HOUSE, often used to indicate one of the major high-street banks.

clearing house a centralized system for settling indebtedness between the financial institutions that are members.

clientele effect the influence of a group of powerful investors who wish an organization to pursue a particular policy.

close company a company of which the SHARE CAPITAL is held or controlled by five or fewer people or by people who are all directors of the company.

closed-end fund a MUTUAL FUND that sells only a certain number of SHARES.

closed shop a company in which there exists an agreement between the employer and a LABOR UNION that only workers who are members of the labor union will be employed.

close price the price of a SHARE or COMMODITY when the difference between the BID PRICE and the offer price is very small.

closing balance the balance, whether debit or

credit, on a LEDGER at the end of a company's accounting period, that will be carried forward to the next accounting period.

closing prices the buying and selling prices that are recorded at the close of a day's trading on the stock market or on a COMMODITY MARKET.

closing stock the stock that remains in a company at the end of an accounting period, including raw materials, WORK IN PROGRESS, or finished products.

CNN effect referring to the effect that news reports have on consumer spending. The terrorist attacks in New York, for example, led to a downturn in air travel as more people stayed home.

code of conduct *or* **code of practice** a set of guidelines indicating what is regarded as acceptable behavior and ethical standards relating to a particular profession or organization.

cold calling a method of selling by which approaches are made by representatives, often by means of door-to-door calls, to people who have not previously shown any interest in the product or service.

collateral an ASSET, such as a LIFE-INSURANCE POLICY, SHARES or the title deeds to a house, that a borrower is required to pledge as security against a LOAN, the asset running the risk of being sold off if the loan is not repaid.

collective bargaining negotiating between employers and representatives of the workforce, such as LABOR UNION negotiators, to establish rates of pay, conditions of employment, etc.

collective wisdom in the STOCK MARKET, the general opinion about the overall value of an investment.

colon 1 the standard monetary unit of Costa Rica, made up of 100 CENTIMOS. **2** the standard monetary unit of El Salvador, made up of 100 CENTAVOS.

commercial bank a bank that provides a wide range of financial services to businesses and to the general public. Such services include receiving deposits, operating checking accounts, offering loan facilities, the supplying of foreign currency, etc.

commercial bill a BILL OF EXCHANGE other than a TREASURY BILL.

commercial draft a demand for payment.

commercial paper short-term unsecured DEBT with a maturity date ranging from two to 270 days. Banks and other financial institutions often raise money by issuing commercial paper to investors.

commission a payment that is made to an intermediary, such as an agent or broker, or to an employee, especially a salesperson, the commission usually being calculated as a percentage of the value of the goods or services sold.

committed costs costs that a company or organization have a long-term commitment to pay. Such costs include the rent on property carrying a long-term lease.

commodity 1 a raw material, such as grain, coffee, tea, wool, etc, that is traded in. **2** any economic GOOD.

commodity broker a broker who deals in COMMODITIES, especially one who trades on behalf of others in the COMMODITY MARKET.

commodity market a market for the trading of COMMODITIES, the main markets being in London and New York. Some commodities are sold at auction but most are exchanged as ACTUALS or FUTURES on commodity exchanges in which dealers are represented by COMMODITY BROKERS.

common stock the owner of a share of common stock in a company can take part in voting for directors and share in the company's PROFITS. However, owners of common stock must take their place behind owners of PREFERRED STOCK when DIVIDENDS are distributed and, usually, to receive ASSETS if the company fails.

commutation the right to receive an instant sum in cash in return for accepting smaller annual payments at some point in the future.

compensation fund (Brit) a fund established by the London Stock Exchange, to which member firms make financial contributions, to provide compensation for those investors who sustain losses as a consequence of a member firm failing to meet a financial obligation.

competition a situation when more than one producer is trying to secure the business of prospective purchasers.

competitive bidding when an offer submitted by a prospective buyer to a seller is in competition with other offers to buy the same product or service.

competitor a company that supplies goods and services similar to those of another company and so is trying to sell to the same range of customers.

competitor analysis the process of studying and assessing the production and marketing methods adopted by a company's key competitors so that the company can establish the nature and extent of its own strengths and weaknesses.

complementary product a product made by a firm that supplements another product or products that it makes. For example a company making envelopes would also make writing paper.

complete portfolio a reference to the PORTFOLIO as a whole, including low, medium and high RISK investments.

compound annual return the total return that is available from an investment in which the interest is employed to increase the investment.

compound interest *see* INTEREST.

compulsory purchase the compulsory acquisition of land or property by the state, usually because the land is necessary for some public use, such as the building of a new road.

concept testing the trying out of a new product or an existing product that has been modified in some way on a sample of likely consumers with a view to assessing consumer reaction to the product.

concert-party agreement (Brit) an agreement between shareholders of a company who are apparently unconnected to act together as a unit to try to influence the management of a company or to influence the share price. The members of the concert party may have bought shares in the company with a view to pooling their holdings and acting together to take over the company.

conciliation a form of intervention in INDUSTRIAL DISPUTES in which a third party tries to assist the two parties involved in the dispute to resolve their differences and reach an agreement that is satisfactory to both of them.

conditional sale agreement a form of contract of sale by which the price of the goods purchased is payable by installments and the seller remains the owner of the goods until they are paid in full, although the goods are in the possession of the purchaser.

Confederation of British Industry (Brit) a non-party organization that represents the collective interest of industry and employers in the UK and aims to promote efficiency and prosperity in British business. There is a central committee and a number of regional and local branches.

conglomerate a group of related companies, often active in diverse and unrelated fields, usually controlled by a HOLDING COMPANY.

conglomerate merger a MERGER between two or more organizations that operate in unrelated fields.

consideration the benefit that a party to a CONTRACT receives when entering into a contractual obligation.

consignee the receiver of a shipment of goods. See also CONSIGNOR.

consignment an arrangement between an exporter and an importer by which the exporter receives payment for goods only when they have been transported and sold by the importer, there often being a considerable delay between the exporter sending the goods and receiving payment.

consignor the sender of a shipment of goods. The consignor is paid by the CONSIGNEE.

consolidation in a company where two or more businesses combine to form a completely new organization. *See also* CONGLOMERATE MERGER.

Consols (Brit) a form of security issued by the government at a fixed price and bearing a nominal fixed interest rate. Consols can be bought and sold on the stock market at prices that vary according to the forces of supply and demand, although they do not carry a specified redemption date.

Consolidated Fund (Brit) in the UK the money that is received by the government in taxes and from which are paid certain items of public expenditure approved by Parliament, like the cost of running the Civil Service. The money is kept by the Bank of England in an account known as the Exchequer Account and is under the control of the Treasury.

consortium a combination of two or more large companies formed for a specific and limited purpose, such as the submitting of a quotation for an exceptionally large project, such as the building of a nuclear power station, on which the companies would then pool resources for the period of the project if the quotation were accepted.

conspicuous consumption a term, invented by the American economist Thorstein Veblen, to describe when people buy and use consumer goods in such a way as to consciously try to impress other people or to display their wealth and status.

consumer a person who purchases and uses goods and services to satisfy his or her needs.

consumer durables goods, such as television sets, refrigerators, cars, etc, that have a useful life that extends over a relatively long period of time, unlike CONSUMER NON-DURABLES.

consumer goods goods, including both CONSUMER DURABLES and CONSUMER NON-DURABLES, that are purchased and used by members of the public.

consumerism a movement that aims to protect the interests of the consumer by trying to ensure that goods conform to the descriptions given on the labels, that goods are safe to consume or use, etc.

consumer non-durables goods, such as food, soap and cleaning materials, that are purchased by members of the public and are used either immediately or within a relatively short time, unlike CONSUMER DURABLES.

Consumer Price Index a gauge of monthly changes in consumer prices based on a survey of housing, food and other costs, compiled by the Bureau of Labor Statistics.

contingency plan a plan formulated by a company that can be put into practice in the event of some circumstance occurring.

contingent liability a liability that may occur if a certain circumstance occurs.

continuous processing a process in which extremely high volumes of a product are produced continuously on plant specifically designed for the purpose. The generation of electricity is an example of continuous processing.

contract an agreement between two or more parties that is legally enforceable.

contract note a document that is sent out by a stockbroker or commodity broker to a client as proof that SECURITIES or COMMODITIES have been bought or sold along the lines of the client's instructions.

contract of employment an agreement by which an employee undertakes to work for an employer for a certain remuneration and which sets out the terms and conditions of employment.

contractor a person or company that enters into a contract to supply goods or services to another person or company.

control the direction of the financial and operational policies of a company, making sure that these are efficient and effective and taking corrective action where necessary. For example, control of expenditure involves the monitoring of budgets and making sure they are within budget targets.

controller the officer responsible for the company's overall accounting activities. This will include general accounting, cost accounting, budgeting, economic forecasting and all matters concerning local, state and Federal taxes. Sometimes written as *comptroller*.

controlling interest a financial interest in a company that gives the person holding the investment control of the company. For example, a shareholder would have the controlling interest in a company if he or she had more than 50 per cent of the voting shares or a considerable number of shares, although less than 50 per cent, if the rest of the shareholding is divided among a large number of people.

conversion cost the costs involved in a production process in which raw material is converted into finished product.

convertibility the extent to which a FINANCIAL SECURITY, such as a foreign currency, can be freely exchanged for another.

convertible currency a currency that can be freely converted into the currency of another country without permission having to be obtained from foreign exchange control authorities.

conveyancing the transfer of ownership of land and buildings from the current owner to a new owner.

cookie jar accounting an accounting method that uses reserves from "good" years to offset losses that may be incurred in "bad" years.

cook the books a colloquial expression in accounting which describes an effort to disguise an organization's true financial position by falsifying records. *See also* CREATIVE ACCOUNTING, AGGRESSIVE ACCOUNTING.

cooperative an organization formed by a group of volunteers to serve their own needs. Each member of the group has an equal vote on operative decisions and profits are shared equally between members.

copyright the legal ownership of certain kinds of material, such as literary, dramatic, artistic and musical works and sound and television broadcasting and films, and the exclusive right to reproduce these or to authorize others to do so. In the case of an author, copyright lasts for 70 years after his or her death. If copyright is infringed the copyright owner may seek legal redress.

cordoba the standard monetary unit of Nicaragua, equal to 100 CENTAVOS.

core holding an important, long-term investment in the owner's PORTFOLIO.

corner a market to buy goods or SECURITIES in large enough amounts to enable the purchaser to manipulate the price.

corporate acquisition the taking over of one firm by another.

corporate governance the manner in which a company is managed and the nature and effectiveness of management responsibility, in particular the accountability of management to the owners or shareholders.

corporate restructuring 1 a change in a company's internal system of organization, for example a move towards greater or less centralization in decision-making. **2** a change in a company's business strategy, for example a move to diversify its business activities or a move to abandon previous business activities.

corporation a business organization registered with the state or Federal government with certain characteristics such as LIMITED LIABILITY for SHAREHOLDERS, easy transfer of ownership and continuity of existence.

corporation tax a tax that is levied on the total profits of a company in each accounting period. In the UK provision is made for smaller companies that pay a lower rate than larger companies.

correspondent bank a bank in a foreign country that provides banking services to the customers of a bank in another country, there usually being a reciprocal agreement between the two banks, particularly for the transmission of money from country to country.

cost 1 expenditure on the purchasing of goods or services. **2** expenditure of a company's resources, usually money, involved in producing and selling its products or in achieving its goals.

cost-benefit analysis a systematic examination of all the costs and benefits that are expected to be derived from a planned course of action.

cost effective a situation where the financial RETURN from a project is greater than the amount invested to set it up.

cost of capital the cost to a company of the capital that is used to finance its business activities. This capital usually includes loans and share capital.

cost of living the amount of money paid by an individual or a family for food, clothing and other essentials necessary to maintain a certain standard of living.

cost-of-living adjustment a wage or salary increase intended to compensate for general rises in the COST OF LIVING. It may also apply to workers who relocate to places where the cost of living is much higher than they are used to.

cost of goods sold an assessment of how much it cost to make the products sold. Such costs include the raw materials, labor, manufacturing, advertising and distribution costs.

couma *see* DRAM.

counterfeit a product produced to imitate the genuine article and passed off as the real thing with the intent to defraud.

countertrading in international trading, the practice of paying for goods by means other than cash, usually by the direct or indirect exchange of goods. Countertrading usually occurs when a foreign currency is in short supply or when countries impose some kind of foreign exchange control.

countervailing power the idea, put forward by the American economist J.K. Galbraith, suggesting that in capitalist economies there is an element of self-regulation because the economic strength of the large corporations is checked by the power of the LABOR UNIONS.

coupon 1 a detachable, dated slip that is attached to a BOND or SHARE certificate and that must be produced in order to claim payment of INTEREST or DIVIDENDS due on the bond or share. **2** the rate of interest that is paid on a fixed-interest security. **3** a slip of paper that is issued to consumers by suppliers as part of a promotional exercise, the coupon, for example, giving the consumer the right to get a product at a reduced rate or get it free, depending on the terms of the promotional deal.

coupon rate a BOND's annual rate of INTEREST expressed as a percentage of what was actually paid for the bond. Also known as *nominal yield*.

covenant a written agreement in the form of a deed by which a person contracts to do something that is then enforceable by law. A common form of covenant is one by which a person agrees to pay a regular sum of money to a charity for a certain period. *See* DEED OF COVENANT.

crash 1 a rapid and serious fall of prices on the stock market. **2** a breakdown of a computer system.

creative accounting a method of accounting that seeks to use all means possible that are not actually illegal to present the financial position of a company in as favourable a light as possible.

creative destruction in business, a process in which a new industry destroys an old one. For example, personal computers destroyed the typewriter industry.

credit 1 the sum of money that a trader will allow a customer to owe him or her before payment is asked for. **2** a financial facility by which a person or company can borrow money to make purchases without paying for the goods bought immediately, the purchasers usually making payments for the goods over an extended period of time. Credit facilities are supplied by banks, finance houses and money-lenders, bank loans, overdrafts and credit cards being common methods of obtaining credit. **3** the financial standing and reputation of a person or company. **4** in accounting, an entry on the right-hand side of an account recording a payment received.

credit control a system operated by a company to make sure that customers pay outstanding debts within a reasonable period of time and to try to minimize the likelihood of incurring bad debts.

credit note a document given to a customer by a supplier giving the customer credit for any goods that have been returned by the customer and for which the supplier has already received payment.

creditor a person or company to whom another person or company owes money, for example in respect of goods or services supplied.

credit rating an assessment of the creditworthiness of a person or company taken as an indication of how safe it is to allow him, her or it credit facilities and what level of credit facilities could be considered to be a safe limit.

credit risk the risk that a borrower may default on a LOAN. A good credit risk is considered less likely to DEFAULT than a bad credit risk.

credit sale a sale involving the extension of credit for payment. See CREDIT 2.

credit terms the conditions under which a CREDIT SALE is made. These usually specify the INTEREST rate charged, the length of time available for payment and how payments are to be made.

critical mass in business, a crucial stage of an organization's development, such as selling its products overseas or expanding into major new premises.

crore in India, Pakistan and Bangladesh, 100 LAKHS.

cross holdings where one firm owns SHARES in another firm.

crown jewels a popular expression for a company's most valuable ASSET. This may make the company the subject of a TAKEOVER BID.

cruzeiro *see* CENTAVO 2.

cumulative preference share a type of PREFERENCE SHARE that allows the owner to receive any DIVIDENDS that were not paid in previous years.

curb trading trading that occurs away from the STOCK MARKET and outside its rules and regulations, often by telephone.

currency 1 the money of a particular country. 2 any kind of money that is in general use as cash, being passed from person to person as coins and banknotes. 3 any generally accepted means of payment used as a medium of exchange, as checks, bills of exchange and promissory notes as well as coins and banknotes. 4

the length of time that has to elapse before a bill of exchange becomes due for payment.

current assets ASSETS, such as STOCK-IN-TRADE, cash, and money owed by debtors, that are used up or turned over fairly soon in the course of the business and production activities of a business.

current liabilities all the liabilities of a company, such as payments due to trade creditors, that are payable at some date in the relatively near future, often within a year of the company's balance sheet date.

current ratio the ratio of the CURRENT ASSETS of a business to the CURRENT LIABILITIES, used as a test of a company's liquidity.

customization the adaptation or development of goods or services to accord with the special requirements of a specific customer.

customs duty a form of tax that is levied by the government on foreign products that are imported into the country.

cut-throat competition a fierce price war between two or more firms that is intended to force competitors out of business. The firm that survives will charge higher prices in future to recoup the losses incurred during the price war.

cyclical fluctuation alternating periods of economic prosperity and recession.

cyclical industry an industry that is vulnerable to

external factors that affect its activities. The construction industry, for example, is a cyclical industry as there is higher activity in the summer than in the winter. The same applies to tourism.

cyclical stock an investment where the value rises rapidly when the economy is strong, but falls equally rapidly when growth slows. Luxury goods are an example of cyclical stock; healthcare is an example of non-cyclical stock, as demand remains relatively constant.

D

daisy chain colloquial expression for a group of investors who fraudulently manipulate the price of a SECURITY so that it is sold at a profit to themselves.

dalasi the standard monetary unit of the Gambia, made up of 100 bututs.

database an organized store of information held on a computer and used in business for a variety of reasons. For example, sales departments use a database to store names and addresses of customers for purposes of mailing lists.

data processing the organization and processing of computerized information, such as company records.

data protection (Brit) protection relating to personal information about individuals that is stored on computer systems. This is governed in the UK by the Data Protection Act (1984), which sets out to protect individuals against abuse of this information. The act has a number of principles, two of the most important being that personal data shall be held only for specified and lawful purposes and shall not be used or disclosed in any manner incompatible with those purposes and that personal data held for any purpose shall not be kept longer than necessary for that purpose.

date of payment the date on which DIVIDEND checks are mailed.

dawn raid an attempt made, often as part of a TAKEOVER BID, to buy a substantial shareholding in the company that is the target of the takeover bid as soon as the STOCK EXCHANGE opens so as to take the directors of the TARGET COMPANY by surprise. The substantial shareholding thus acquired then acts as a platform for the full takeover bid to take place.

days of grace the extra time that is granted for payment of an INSURANCE PREMIUM or BILL OF EXCHANGE after the due date.

dealer 1 a trader of any kind. **2** a person who deals for himself or herself as a PRINCIPAL on the STOCK EXCHANGE rather than as an AGENT or BROKER.

dead cat bounce in the STOCK MARKET, a small upward price movement in a BEAR market. (Refers to the saying that even a dead cat will bounce if it's dropped from a great enough height!)

debenture a common method of providing CAPITAL for companies through long-term LOANS often secured against company ASSETS.

debit an entry on the left-hand or debtor side of a double-entry company accounts. *See* DOUBLE-ENTRY BOOK-KEEPING.

debit note a document that is sent by a company to an organization or individual indicating the cost of products or services supplied and as yet not paid for.

debt a sum that is owed by one company, individual etc, to another.

debt collection agency an organization that is responsible for the collection of the outstanding debts of its clients, the agency being commissioned in return for collecting the money owed.

debtor a company or individual that owes money to another.

debt ratio a way of measuring an organization's stability, such as by finding the ratio between total DEBT and NET WORTH.

decimal currency a form of currency in which the standard monetary unit is subdivided into 100 parts. Decimal currency was introduced into the UK in 1971.

declaration date the date on which a company's board of directors declare or announce the date and amount of the next DIVIDEND payment.

deductions at source a form of tax collection in which a person who is paying money to another for work carried out deducts INCOME TAX from the money paid before giving the money to the employee and is responsible for paying the tax to the tax authorities.

deed a document that has been signed, sealed and

delivered. Some transactions by law have to be carried out by means of a deed rather than other document in order to be valid.

deed of trust a legal instrument by which title to REAL ESTATE is passed to a trustee to hold as SECURITY for something. Only a qualified attorney should prepare a deed of trust.

de facto (Latin) "existing in fact." Something may not be moral, legal or officially recognized, but it exists all the same. See also DE JURE.

defalcation embezzlement by a person in a position of trust. Organizations often take out an indemnity bond to protect themselves against such an occurrence.

default failure to carry out the terms of a CONTRACT.

deferred annuity a form of ANNUITY in which payments do not begin right away but begin either at a specified date in the future or when the policyholder reaches a specified age.

deficit any shortfall of CASH, such as would occur with more CREDITORS than DEBTORS or more operating LOSSES than PROFITS.

deflation a fall in the level of the general prices in an economy, the opposite of INFLATION.

degearing the process by which some of the loan stock of a company is replaced by ORDINARY SHARE capital.

de jure (Latin) "existing according to law." See also DE FACTO.

delivery note a document, usually in duplicate, that is sent by a supplier to a customer when goods are delivered. The delivery note itemizes the goods and is signed by the customer as proof of delivery.

demand curve a line on a chart indicating the relationship between the price of a product and the quantity of a product demanded.

demand deposit account an account that allows funds to be withdrawn, for example by writing a check, without clearing the transaction with the bank first.

demand-pull inflation a rise in prices caused by an excess of demand over supply

demand shock an unforeseen event that affects consumer demand. *See also* CNN EFFECT.

demarcation dispute an industrial dispute based on the allocation of tasks in a workplace. There are often several unions representing different occupational groups in a large workplace and they are anxious to observe the demarcation lines that set off the work that should be done by one trade from that which should be done by another, although sometimes the demarcation lines are not always clear.

demerger the break-up of one company, often one that has been formed by MERGER, into two or more separate companies.

demographic segmentation the division of a market into SOCIO-ECONOMIC GROUPS according to such demographic variables as age, sex, occupation, education, income, etc.

deposit account an account with a financial institution from which money cannot be withdrawn by CHECK, such as a savings account with a SAVINGS AND LOAN ASSOCIATION.

depository transfer check (DTC) a check paid directly by a bank to a particular firm or person.

depreciation 1 the reduction in value of an asset during the course of its operative life, caused, for example, by use or by OBSOLESCENCE. **2** the reduction in value of the currency of one country against another.

depression a severe form of RECESSION.

deregulation the removal of certain controls on an area of economic activity that have been imposed by the government or some other regulatory body.

Deutschmark the former standard monetary unit of Germany, made up of 100 PFENNIG, and replaced by the Euro on January 1 2002.

devaluation a reduction in the exchange rate of one currency against another.

development costs costs incurred by a company in making improvements to a product or process marketed by it.

development stage in business, that stage of a company's life when it is concentrating mainly on RESEARCH AND DEVELOPMENT. PROFITS, consequently, are generally negligible during this period. An example of a company undergoing its development stage would be a pharmaceutical company researching new drugs and treatments.

dialing and smiling a sales technique in which people, who have shown no previous interest in a product or service, are called by a member of a sales team who attempts to sell them goods or services by telephone. Sales people are encouraged to adopt an open, friendly tone of voice to promote trust. *See also* COLD CALLING.

differentiated marketing *same as* PRODUCT DIFFERENTIATION.

dilution of equity a decrease in earnings from SHARES and a reduction in control experienced by existing shareholders in a company when new shares are issued to attract new shareholders.

dinar 1 the standard monetary unit of Algeria, made up of 100 CENTIMES. **2** the standard monetary unit of Bahrain, Iraq, Jordan, Kuwait and Yemen, made up of 1000 FILS. **3** the standard monetary unit of Tunisia, made up of 1000 milimes. **4** the standard monetary unit of Libya, made up of 1000 DIRHAMS. **5** a monetary unit of Iran, equal to one hundredth of a RIAL. **6** the standard monetary unit of Bosnia-Herzegovina and Serbia, made up of 100 PARAS.

dink a slang acronym for "dual income, no kids," describing a married couple who are both employed but have no children. Such a couple are likely to have more disposable income that a couple with children.

direct costs *or* **prime costs** costs incurred by a company that can be directly traced to the production of a particular product or service. Direct costs are usually made up of DIRECT LABOR, DIRECT MATERIALS and direct expenses.

direct debit (Brit) an order given to a bank by an account-holder to pay regular amounts from his or her account to an organization or individual. Unlike a STANDING ORDER, the amount to be paid under the terms of the direct debit is not specified, this perhaps being subject to variation from one year to another.

direct labor workers in a company who are directly concerned with the production of a product or service. *See* DIRECT COSTS.

direct-mail selling a form of DIRECT MARKETING in which sales and advertising literature is sent directly to a series of selected potential customers.

direct marketing a method of marketing in which the seller deals directly with the consumers rather than through a RETAILER.

direct materials materials that are directly incorporated in a particular product made by a company and so their cost is included in DIRECT COSTS.

direct quote in FOREIGN EXCHANGE, the number of US dollars required to buy one unit of a foreign currency.

director a person who is appointed to carry out the management of a company. There are usually several directors and together they form a BOARD OF DIRECTORS. EXECUTIVE DIRECTORS are directors who have salaried management posts in the company while NON-EXECUTIVE DIRECTORS are not employed by the company but provide advice and expertise in return for directors' fees.

dirham 1 the standard monetary unit of Morocco, made up of 100 CENTIMES. **2** the standard monetary unit of the United Arab Emirates, made up of 100 FILS. **3** a monetary unit of Qatar, equal to one hundredth of a RIYAL. **4** a monetary unit of Libya equal to one thousandth of a DINAR.

disclaimer of opinion a statement made by an AUDITOR declining to put forward any opinion at all on a company's financial situation. *See also* AUDITOR'S REPORT.

discount 1 a reduction in the list price of goods. Such discounts occur for various reasons. Examples include discounts for bulk-buying, discounts for cash payment or prompt payment, discounts to members of a particular trade, club, etc, discounts during an end-of-season sale, etc. **2** the amount by which the market price of a financial security is below its PAR VALUE. **3** a deduction from a BILL OF EXCHANGE when it is purchased before its MATURITY DATE.

discount house a financial institution that specializes in the buying and selling of BILLS OF EXCHANGE and government treasury bills.

discount period the time during which a DISCOUNT may be deducted from the total amount of a bill when making payment.

discount rate the interest rate at which future cash inflows and cash outflows associated with a particular investment project are discounted in order to allow for the timing of these CASH FLOWS.

discount store a retail store, usually a self-service store, that routinely sells a range of standard products at discounted prices, i.e. prices that are considerably less than the manufacturers' SUGGESTED RETAIL PRICES.

disposable income the income that a person has available to spend after the usual deductions, such as TAX and PENSION contributions, have been removed from his or her salary or wage.

distribution 1 the process of storing products and delivering them to customers, often through the medium of wholesalers and retailers. **2** the division of property and ASSETS according to a legal procedure, such as the allocation of the property and assets of a deceased person or of a bankrupt person.

distribution channel the network used in the distribution of a product from the manufacture to the customer.

distributor one of the intermediaries, such as a wholesaler, in the DISTRIBUTION CHANNEL of a product.

diversification the expansion of a company into a different or wider range of products than those that the company usually produces. This is usually undertaken by a company to avoid reliance on one market, particularly a market that seems vulnerable for some reason.

divestment the selling off or closure by a firm of part of its operation.

dividend a payment made by a company to its shareholders for providing the SHARE CAPITAL to enable the company to carry on its business. Dividends are paid in proportion to the number of shares held and are a proportion of the after-tax profit of a company, the remaining profit being reinvested in the company's business operations.

dividend warrant the check that is issued to a shareholder in payment of a DIVIDEND. The warrant states the net amount paid and the amount of tax that has been deducted.

divisionalization the breaking-up of an organization into separate divisions, based on differences of product or services, geographical location, etc.

dobra the standard monetary unit of São Tomé e Principe, made up of 100 CENTAVOS.

dog eat dog an expression that describes a ruthlessly competitive market where firms offering similar products or services attempt to undercut each other by means of techniques such as sales, "2 for 1" and money back offers.

dollar the standard monetary unit of Antigua and Barbuda, Australia, Barbados, Belize, Bermuda, British Virgin Islands, Brunei, Canada, Cayman Islands, Dominica, Fiji, Grenada, Guam, Guyana, Hong Kong, Jamaica, Kiribati, Liberia, New Zealand, Puerto Rico, St Kitts and Nevis, Singapore, the Solomon Islands, Taiwan, Trinidad and Tobago, the USA, US Virgin Islands and Zimbabwe, made up of 100 cents.

dollar-cost-averaging a system in which an investor buys SECURITIES at regular intervals in fixed dollar amounts. So the investor buys fewer SHARES when prices are high and more shares when prices are low. Over time, therefore, the investor will pay a lower average purchase price per share.

Domestic International Sales Corporation (DISC) an American organization that is responsible for promoting exports.

domestic market a country's home or internal market.

dong *see* HAO, TRINH, XU.

dormant account in banking, a bank account that has been set up but is not being used or a bank account that has been inactive for a long time.

dotcom a company that relies on the internet for a major part of its business. The so-called "dotcom boom" hit the world in the late 1990s when dozens of companies sprang into life, many of them based in SILICON VALLEY, California. Most of these companies were hugely overvalued on the STOCK MARKET and within a few years had crashed. *See also* SILICONAIRES.

double barreled in the STOCK MARKET, BONDS that are secured by more than one source of repayment.

double-entry book-keeping a method of recording business transactions between a company and outside firms that involves recording both aspects of each transaction – what is paid out and what is received. For example, when a debtor pays cash to a company for goods or services supplied, the record of cash held by the company is increased by the relevant amount and the amount of money due from the debtor is decreased by that amount. The double-entry system is a reliable system of account control as both entry-systems have to balance against each other.

double taxation taxation on income and profit in more than one country, the country in which they are earned and the country to which the income and profit is remitted.

doubtful debts money that is owed to a company but that it is unlikely ever to receive.

Dow Jones Industrial Average an index of share prices that is issued by Dow Jones & Co, an American firm that supplies financial information, and is used on the New York Stock Exchange. It is comparable to the London FINANCIAL TIMES ORDINARY SHARE INDEX.

downside in the STOCK MARKET, an estimated amount by which a market or stock could fall expressed in dollars. For example, "The potential downside on company XYZ is $10," means that this company's stock may fall by $10 a share.

downside risk the assessment of how much a project would cost if it failed.

downsizing the reduction of the size of a company, especially in terms of the number of workers employed, in order to decrease costs and perhaps increase flexibility.

downstream a term used in industries such as oil

and gas, to refer to that stage when a company has completed its exploration and production phases and oil or gas is now being sold. Most oil and gas companies are "integrated", combining both downstream and UPSTREAM activities.

downtime the period of time during which a computer or piece of machinery is not operational.

drachma the former standard monetary unit of Greece, made up of 100 LEPTA, replaced by the Euro on January 1 2002.

dragon bond an Asian BOND with its value expressed in US dollars.

dram the standard monetary unit of Armenia, made up of 100 couma.

drill-bit stock in the STOCK MARKET, refers to SHARES that trade for prices lower than $1.

dry powder (slang) refers to an amount of CASH kept by a company in reserve to pay for possible future LIABILITIES.

due date the date on which a debt of some kind is due to be settled.

due diligence in business, the reasonable amount of care a person or institution should take before entering into a transaction. *See also* CAVEAT EMPTOR.

dumbbell an investment strategy that includes both short and long-term MATURITIES in the PORTFOLIO. *Also known as* BARBELL STRATEGY.

dummy director a member of a board of directors who acts according to the wishes of someone who is not a board member.

dummy shareholder a person who has SHARES registered in his or her name, although the shares actually belong to someone else. BROKERS may hold shares on behalf of a client in order to conceal their true ownership.

dumping the process of selling goods on the export market at a price well below that charged on the domestic market.

Dutch auction an auction where the price of a product is reduced until an offer is made for it, when it is sold at that price. In investing, US TREASURY SECURITIES are sold in this way.

duty a government tax that is levied on certain goods or services.

E

E & OE the abbreviation for **errors and omissions excepted**, which is often printed on invoice forms to protect the interests of the sender of the invoice in case an error has been introduced in the recipient's favor.

early adopter one of a group of consumers who begin to use a new product very soon after it has been put on the market but who are not among the very first customers who are pioneers of the new product.

earned Income income that is earned from employment or self-employment, as opposed to UN-EARNED INCOME, which is derived from the ownership of ASSETS, such as INTEREST and DIVIDENDS from investments, rents from property, etc.

earnings the NET INCOME of a person or an organization during a given period.

earnings per share the NET PROFIT after tax that is attributable to each ORDINARY SHARE in a company. It is calculated by dividing the total net profit after tax by the number of ordinary shares.

earnings yield the NET PROFIT after tax per ORDINARY SHARE (EARNINGS PER SHARE) for a specified accounting period expressed as a percentage of the current market price per share.

earn-out agreement an agreement to buy a company, under which the buyer agrees to pay a lump sum at the time of purchase but agrees to a contingency agreement by which a larger amount will be paid if certain criteria are met during a specified number of years after purchase.

EC abbreviation for ECONOMIC COMMUNITY.

e-commerce used to describe a business that uses the internet as a major part of its function. Almost anything can now be bought and sold over the internet. *See also* DOTCOM.

econometrics the employment of statistical techniques in the analysis of economic data.

economic assumptions the assumptions that are made about the future general economic situation when an organization is planning its forthcoming financial strategy.

economic growth an increase in the output of a country's economy in terms of goods and services.

economic life the period of time during which an ASSET, such as a piece of machinery, can be used effectively or profitably.

economic sanctions restriction on imports or exports imposed on a country by another country or group of countries in order to cause damage to its economic interests and so bring pressure on it to bring about political or social change.

economic value the present value of expected future CASH FLOWS.

economies of scale reductions in the average cost of production, and thus in unit costs, when production output has been increased. Such economies enable the producer to offer more competitive prices.

ECU the abbreviation for EUROPEAN CURRENCY UNIT.

EDGAR (Brit) the abbreviation for Electronic Data Gathering and Retrieval, a system used by the Securities and Exchange Commission (*see* SEC) to send reports etc. to investors.

effective tax rate the average tax rate that is applicable in a given situation.

efficiency in business, the ability to minimize wasted time, energy and resources in the production of goods and services.

efficient capital market in the STOCK MARKET, a market where new information is rapidly reflected in SHARE prices.

EFTA the abbreviation for EUROPEAN FREE TRADE ASSOCIATION.

EFTPOS the abbreviation for ELECTRONIC FUNDS TRANSFER AT POINT OF SALE.

elephants a reference to very large organizations, such as banks and pension funds, that invest huge amounts in the STOCK MARKET and can therefore have a major influence on market prices.

electronic data interchange an electronic data-transmission system that enables firms to exchange business documents, such as orders and invoices, by electronic means rather than by hard copy.

electronic funds transfer at point of sale when a purchase is made the automatic debiting of a customer's bank account or credit-card account using a computer link between the check-out till and the bank or credit-card company.

electronic mail *or* **e-mail** *or* **email** a form of electronic communication by which computer originated messages can be sent by means of a telecommunication network and a modem. Each e-mail user has an e-mail address

electronic point of sale an electronic system of recording purchases in retail outlets. The system records the total amount to be paid by the purchaser and provides an itemized customer receipt, a scanner having been used to decode the BAR CODES on items. It also automatically adjusts the firm's stock records.

electronic shopping a form of electronic DIRECT MARKETING by which consumers can make purchases from a computerized list on a screen by means of a cable or telephone link to the seller.

electronic transfer of funds the electronic transfer of money from one bank account to another by means of computers and telecommunication links.

eligible list (Brit) a list of the names of banks that are allowed to discount acceptances at the Bank of England.

e-mail *or* **email** the abbreviation for ELECTRONIC MAIL.

embargo a ban on trade with a country or group of countries or on particular products. This is a form of ECONOMIC SANCTION.

emerging markets growing financial markets in developing countries.

emoluments the total amount of financial benefit from an employment or office, including salary, fee or wage, expenses and perquisites.

employee participation the participation by the workforce in the decision-making processes. The participation may take several forms. For example, a representative of the employees of a company might be appointed to the board of directors of a company or shares might be allocated to employees.

employee stock ownership plan (ESOP) a system that allows employees to buy SHARES in the company they work for. Employees may then take part in the management and development of the company.

employers' liability insurance a form of insurance, compulsory by law, that covers an employer's legal liability to pay compensation to employees in the event of injury or death at work.

employment agency an agency that maintains a list of employment vacancies as provided by prospective employers and a list of people seeking work and acts as an agent between the two. The agency may also interview the prospective employees on behalf of the employer, act as a recruiting agency and provide temporary staff. The owners of the agency usually charge the employers a fee for the service.

empowerment the allotting of increased responsibility and a degree of control to employees with a view to increasing their levels of JOB SATISFACTION and increasing motivation.

endowment (funds) money or other valuables gifted to an organization such as a school or hospital, in order to provide income for its operation and development.

endowment policy an INSURANCE POLICY that matures at a stated time when the insured person is paid the agreed sum insured. If the insured person dies before maturity, a named beneficiary is paid the FACE VALUE of the policy.

EMS the abbreviation for EUROPEAN MONETARY SYSTEM.

EMU the abbreviation for EUROPEAN MONETARY UNION.

enterprise a business venture, usually carrying an element of RISK.

enterprise investment scheme (Brit) an investment scheme, introduced in the UK in 1994, by which tax relief is available on eligible shares in an unquoted company that has been trading for three years.

enterprise zone an area, usually of relatively high employment, designated by the government in which certain financial inducements are offered to companies that are prepared to make new investment in the area.

entrepot trade a form of international trading in which goods are temporarily imported into a country and then re-exported.

entrepreneur a person who invests in a new business and bears the risk associated with that investment.

Environmental Protection Agency (EPA) a Federal government agency established in 1970 to protect the environment by monitoring waste disposal and controlling pollution.

EPOS the abbreviation for ELECTRONIC POINT OF SALE.

Equal Employment Opportunity Commission (EEOC) a Federal government agency that deals with discrimination issues in the workplace.

equal pay the right of men and women to be paid the same rate of pay for performing the same job or work of equal value.

equity 1 the NET ASSETS of a company after all debts and liabilities have been paid. **2** the ORDINARY SHARE capital of a company. **3** the amount of money that is returned to a borrower in a MORTGAGE or other loan agreement after the asset involved has been sold and the full repayment of the sum lent. **4** the value of an asset after the deduction of any liabilities outstanding on it.

ergonomics the study of the relation of workers to their working environment with a view to maximizing efficiency and providing safe, comfortable working conditions.

ERM *see* EXCHANGE RATE MECHANISM.

errors and omissions excepted *see* E & OE.

escalation clause a clause in a CONTRACT, usually one concerned with long-term work, that gives authorization to a contractor to increase the contracted price under certain specified conditions.

escape clause a clause in a CONTRACT that allows for the release of one party from all or part of the obligations imposed by the contract under certain specified conditions.

escrow a deed that has been signed and sealed but will be delivered on the condition that it will not become operative until the occurrence of some stated later event and that it cannot be revoked in the meantime.

escudo 1 the standard monetary unit of Madeira

and Cape Verde, being made up of 100 CENTAVOS. **2** the former standard currency of Portugal, replaced by the Euro on January 1 2002.

estate the total of a person's ASSETS minus his or her LIABILITIES as valued on death or for the purposes of INHERITANCE TAX.

estate duty formerly a tax payable on the ESTATE of a deceased person. *See* INHERITANCE TAX.

ethical investment an investment made in a company that is not engaged in business activity that the investor considers to be unethical, such as armaments, or is engaged in a business activity that the investor considers to be of a particularly ethical nature, such as something that will be of help in improving or preserving the environment.

ethics standards of conduct and moral principles applied to behavior and action.

euro the currency unit used in the EUROPEAN MONETARY UNION.

Eurobond a BOND that pays INTEREST in EURODOLLARS.

Euro CDs CDs issued by a US bank branch or foreign bank in another country. Most Euro CDs originate in London.

eurocurrency a currency held in a European country other than its country of origin. For example, dollars that are deposited in a European bank are known as EURODOLLARS.

Eurodollar bonds EUROBONDS issued in EURODOL-LARS.

Eurodollars US dollars deposited in a European bank or in a US bank branch in Europe.

European Commission the body that administers the work of the EUROPEAN UNION.

European Community *see* EUROPEAN ECONOMIC COMMUNITY.

European Currency Unit (abbreviated to **ECU**) a currency medium and unit of account that was established in 1979 to act as the accounting unit and reserve asset of the EUROPEAN MONETARY SYSTEM.

European Economic Community an association of Western European countries formed under the terms of the Treaty of Rome of 1957 to establish a common market among its members. Initially there were six members – Belgium, France, Italy, Luxembourg, the Netherlands and West Germany. These were joined in 1973 by the United Kingdom, Denmark and Ireland, by which time it had become known as the European Community, and later by Greece, Spain and Portugal. Austria, Sweden and Finland joined in 1995, by which time the organization had developed into the EUROPEAN UNION. In 2004, Poland, Estonia, Latvia, Lithuania, the Czech Republic, Slovakia, Hungary, Slovenia, Malta and Cyprus joined as new members bringing some 72 million new citizens into the union.

European Economic Area an organization formed in 1991 between members of the European Community, later the EUROPEAN UNION and the EUROPEAN FREE TRADE ASSOCIATION.

European Free Trade Association a trade association established in 1960 between Austria, Denmark, Norway, Portugal, Sweden, Switzerland and the UK. Finland, Iceland and Liechtenstein joined later. In 1973 the UK and Denmark left to join the EUROPEAN COMMUNITY and Portugal joined them in 1986.

European Monetary Union (abbreviated to **EMU**) a system, agreed by the participating countries in the MAASTRICHT TREATY of 1991 by which the members of the EUROPEAN COMMUNITY will have a single European currency, the EURO, and a European central bank.

European Monetary System (abbreviated to **EMS**) a system established in 1979 to coordinate and stabilize the exchange rates of the member countries of the EUROPEAN COMMUNITY.

European Union an association of European countries created in 1993 from the EUROPEAN COMMUNITY, with the aim of providing close economic, social and political links among its members.

Euroyen bonds EUROBONDS denominated in Japanese YEN.

evergreen loan in US banking, this indicates a short-term LOAN that, instead of being repaid, is continually being renewed.

exceptional items see EXTRAORDINARY ITEMS.

excess capacity *same as* OVERCAPACITY.

exchange the marketplace where BONDS, STOCKS and SHARES are bought and sold. The main US exchanges are NEW YORK STOCK EXCHANGE (NYSE), AMERICAN STOCK EXCHANGE (AMEX) and the NATIONAL ASSOCIATION OF SECURITIES DEALERS (NASDAQ).

exchange controls government restrictions on the buying and selling of foreign and domestic currencies in order to protect the value of the country's currency.

exchange rate the official value of one country's currency in relation to the currency of another country.

exchange rate mechanism (abbreviated to **ERM**) a system under which participating countries of the EUROPEAN UNION undertake to commit themselves to maintain the values of their currencies within agreed limits. Under the exchange rate mechanism, each country's currency is given a fixed central PAR VALUE specified in terms of the European Currency Unit (ECU) and the exchange rate between currencies can move to a restricted degree around these par values.

exchange rate risk the risk that an investment's value may change because of a fluctuating EX-CHANGE RATE.

Exchange, The a nickname for the NEW YORK STOCK EXCHANGE, located in WALL STREET in New York City.

excise tax a TAX that is imposed on a certain act, occupation, sale or use of goods and services, such as gasoline and alcoholic drinks.

exclusive distribution a distribution system in which a distributor carries the goods of only one manufacturer and not those of competing manufacturers or in which only one retailer or wholesaler is allowed to sell a manufacturer's goods in a particular area.

ex-dividend the buyer of SHARES described as "ex-dividend" does not have the right to receive the next declared DIVIDEND which will be taken by the seller.

executive director a director of a company who is also an employee, usually a full-time employee, of that company. Often an executive director will play a specific role on the BOARD OF DIRECTORS, reflecting his or her work in the company, such as marketing director, production director, etc.

executor a person who is named in a will to carry out the task of gathering in any assets relating to the estate of the deceased, discharging any liabilities and distributing any remaining assets to the beneficiaries named in the will.

ex factory *see* EX WORKS.

exit strategy the method by which an investor (such as a VENTURE CAPITALIST) plans to withdraw from an investment he or she has made.

exit value the market price of an asset at the date of a balance sheet less the selling price, making it the NET REALIZABLE VALUE.

expected future return the anticipated RETURN that an investment will give in the future.

expenditure tax a tax on the expenditure of individuals. It is an INDIRECT TAX that is added to the selling price of goods or services. Examples of expenditure tax include EXCISE TAX and CUSTOMS DUTY.

expense 1 a sum spent for goods or services in a company that is normally set against profit in the PROFIT AND LOSS ACCOUNT, being chargeable to the trading activities of a company. **2** money spent by an employee in the course of his or her work for a company and subject to refund by the company.

expert system a computer program that simulates the knowledge, skill and experience of a technical expert in a particular field.

expired costs costs the advantages of which are used up during a current accounting period and which thus do not get carried over to the next accounting period in the form of closing stock or a prepayment.

Export-Import Bank (Ex-Im Bank) a Federal agency that makes LOANS to companies and foreign governments to maintain and increase IMPORTS and EXPORTS.

exports goods or services that are sold to buyers in foreign countries, thus bringing in foreign earnings and contributing to the GROSS NATIONAL PRODUCT.

expropriation official government seizure of private property, sanctioned by international law and taken in the public interest. Compensation is usually paid.

ex-rights SHARES that are traded without the RIGHTS attached.

extraordinary general meeting any general meeting of a company or association other than the ANNUAL GENERAL MEETING.

extraordinary items costs or income that do not stem from the normal, routine activities of the company and that affect a company's PROFIT AND LOSS ACCOUNT. Such items are disclosed after the normal profit or loss has been shown. Extraordinary items must be distinguished from **exceptional items**. The latter do stem from the normal, routine activities of the company and are exceptional only in the largeness or smallness of their amounts.

external audit an AUDIT of a company carried out by an auditor who is not part of the organization but is an independent auditor who works outside the firm.

external growth a form of business growth in which expansion comes not from internal, organic growth but from external business activities such as MERGERS or takeovers.

ex warehouse a term indicating delivery terms for goods in which the purchaser pays for the delivery of the goods but the seller pays the loading charges for road or rail transport.

ex works *or* **ex factory** a term indicating delivery terms for goods in which the purchaser has to pay for transporting them from the factory, although in some cases the seller will pay the loading charges for road or rail transport.

eyrir a monetary unit of Iceland, equal to one hundredth of a KRONA.

F

face value 1 the nominal value, also known as PAR VALUE, that is printed on the face of a security and that may either exceed the MARKET VALUE or be less than it. **2** the value that is printed on a banknote or coin.

factoring the purchasing of the trade debts of a company in order to provide it with enough finance with which to operate (WORKING CAPITAL).

failure costs the cost to a manufacturer of goods that are defective. **Internal failure costs** are the result of defects that have been sustained by the goods during the production process. These either have to be scrapped, with a consequent loss of revenue, or have to incur the cost of being reworked or repaired until they meet the required standard. Alternatively, the goods have to be sold as defective at a discounted price that brings in less revenue.

Fair Labor Standards Act a Federal law protecting workers. In particular, it established the minimum wage and 40-hour week.

fair market value the price of a product or service accepted by a willing seller and a willing buyer.

fair-trade agreement an agreement between manufacturer and retailer that the retailer will sell a specific product at or above an agreed retail price.

fallen angel in the STOCK MARKET, describing a STOCK whose value has dropped dramatically from a previously unprecedented high.

falling knife in the STOCK MARKET, describing a STOCK whose value is falling quickly and dramatically.

false advertising any statement from an advertiser that is untrue or intended to mislead.

family brand a group of BRAND NAMES for the products of a company in which the names contain the same word.

FASB *See* FINANCIAL ACCOUNTING STANDARDS BOARD.

fast market in the STOCK MARKET, indicates an unstable, volatile atmosphere accompanied by heavy trading.

FCIA *See* FOREIGN CREDIT INSURANCE ASSOCIATION.

FDA *See* FOOD AND DRUG ADMINISTRATION.

FDIC *See* FEDERAL DEPOSIT INSURANCE CORPORATION.

feasibility study an analysis of a proposed project to decide whether it is practical and profitable.

featherbedding in labor relations, the practice of reducing output or insisting on more workers than necessary to do a particular task in order to protect jobs. Featherbedding results in excessive costs.

Federal Deposit Insurance Corporation (FDIC) a Federal agency that insures bank depositors' accounts for up to $100,000. If the bank fails, depositors can get their money back. All banks belonging to the FEDERAL RESERVE SYSTEM must belong to the Federal Deposit Insurance Corporation.

Federal Home Loan Banks the agencies that regulate SAVINGS AND LOAN ASSOCIATIONS.

Federal Home Loan Mortgage Corporation (Freddie Mac) a public corporation that buys MORTGAGES from financial institutions and resells them as SECURITIES.

Federal Reserve Bank one of the twelve banks that form the FEDERAL RESERVE SYSTEM in the USA.

Federal Reserve Board the governing body of the FEDERAL RESERVE SYSTEM. The seven members of the Board are appointed by the President of the United States and serve terms of 14 years.

Federal Reserve System the organization consisting of twelve banks situated in various cities in the USA which acts as the central bank of the USA.

fen *see* YUAN.

fiat money money that has been declared by a government to be LEGAL TENDER, although it has no intrinsic value and is not backed by government reserves.

fidelity bonus a business reward accorded to loyal

customers by a supplier. The reward takes various forms, such as access to supplies in times of product shortage, exceptionally prompt delivery times, etc.

fiduciary issue (Brit) the portion of the issue of banknotes by the Bank of England that is backed not by gold but by government securities.

field warehouse a warehouse rented by a firm on another firm's property.

fill or kill order a trading order that will be canceled unless fulfilled within a stipulated time.

FIFO the abbreviated form of FIRST-IN-FIRST-OUT.

filler a monetary unit of Hungary, equal to one hundredth of a FORINT.

fils 1 a monetary unit of Bahrain, Iraq, Jordan and Kuwait, equal to one thousandth of a DINAR. **2** a monetary unit of the United Arab Emirates, equal to one hundredth of a DIRHAM. **3** a monetary unit of Yemen, equal to one hundredth of a RIYAL and one thousandth of a DINAR.

final accounts a company's financial accounts, including the PROFIT AND LOSS ACCOUNT and BALANCE SHEET, prepared at the end of its FISCAL YEAR. These must be audited.

finance house a financial institution that specializes in the supply of instalment credit to borrowers and is often owned by a commercial bank.

Financial Accounting Standards Board (FASB) an independent organization responsible for setting accounting standards and principles for US firms.

financial plan a strategy for the financial future of a firm.

financial security a means of borrowing money and raising new capital issued by companies and financial organizations. Financial securities include SHARES, STOCK, BONDS, DEBENTURES, BILLS OF EXCHANGE, etc.

Financial Times Share Index (Brit) a number of share indexes that are published by the *Financial Times* newspaper as a guide to share prices generally on the London Stock Exchange.

first-in-first-out (abbreviated to **FIFO**) a system of valuing units of raw material, components or finished products issued from stock that is based on the principle of using the earliest unit value as a means of pricing the issues until all the stock at that price has been used up. After that, the next latest price is used for pricing the issues, and so on.

fiscal referring to financial matters.

fiscal policy that part of a company's structure that concerns financial matters. In government, refers to government spending and taxation.

fiscal year an accounting period of 12 consecutive

months that ends with the last day of any month except December.

fishbone chart a chart that shows the various constituent operations that are used in the manufacture of products. By means of such a chart it is easier to identify the source of any defect in the product.

Five C's of Credit the standard against which a client's creditworthiness is assessed: Character, Capital, Capacity, Conditions and Collateral.

fixed asset *or* **capital asset** an ASSET, such as buildings, land, plant and machinery, that is used long-term in the trade or business of a company rather than for resale. The costs of such assets are usually written off against the profits of a company over the period of their expected useful life, by allowing for DEPRECIATION each year.

fixed charge a business expense, such as rent, that stays relatively constant and must be paid whether anything is produced or not.

fixed cost an operating expense that does not vary with changes in output, such as an insurance premium; a cost that must be paid whether anything is produced or not.

fixed exchange rate an EXCHANGE RATE between one currency and another that is fixed by government and that is maintained by that government by the buying or selling of its currency where this is necessary to support or lower the value of its currency.

fixed overheads INDIRECT COSTS, the level of which does not vary with the level of production output or sales. Fixed overheads include rent, administration and depreciation of FIXED ASSETS.

fixed-rate loan a LOAN on which the INTEREST is fixed for the lifetime of the loan.

flexible budget a firm's budget which is designed to alter in line with the level of business activity that is actually achieved.

flexitime a system of organizing work hours that allows for a degree of flexibility, particularly in the times of starting and finishing work, provided an agreed number of hours are worked over a period of time, such as a week or month.

floater policy an insurance policy covering goods against loss wherever they are transported or wherever they may be located.

floating exchange rate an EXCHANGE RATE between currencies that is not fixed but that is allowed to float or vary according to MARKET FORCES.

floating capital funds available to a company for general expenses.

flowchart a chart that is used to show the sequence of production operations or flow of material in a production process.

FOB the abbreviation for FREE ON BOARD.

focus group a group of people, led by a MODERATOR,

who are appointed to carry out a detailed discussion and to give views on a particular topic or concept.

Food and Drug Administration (FDA) a Federal government agency that regulates the sale of foods, medicines etc.

Footsie (Brit) a reference to the FTSE100 Index, the 100 established (or BLUE CHIP COMPANIES) that trade on the London Stock Exchange. *See also* DOW JONES INDUSTRIAL AVERAGE, FINANCIAL TIMES SHARE INDEX.

force majeure risk an unforeseeable event that could affect a business project for an indeterminate time, such as fire or storm damage, war, ACT OF GOD or strike.

foreclosure the process by which a MORTGAGOR repossesses a property due to the MORTGAGEE'S inability to pay the MORTGAGE or LOAN secured on the property.

Foreign Credit Insurance Association (FCIA) an organization made up of US INSURANCE companies that offers insurance facilities for exporters.

foreign exchange the currency of foreign countries.

foreign exchange controls controls exercised by the government of a country over the buying and selling of foreign currencies by residents, or the buying and selling of that country's own currency by nonresidents.

foreign exchange dealer a company or person that buys and sells FOREIGN EXCHANGE. The dealer makes his or her money on the difference between the buying and the selling prices.

foreign exchange market an international market in which foreign currencies are bought and sold.

foreign investment investment in a country's domestic economy by foreign companies or individuals. This can take the form of direct investment in manufacturing, etc, or in the form of share investment.

forensic accounting uses accounting, auditing and detective skills to examine a company's finances. Forensic accountants are frequently employed in fraud cases and produce an accounting analysis for use in court.

forfeiture the loss of right to a property as a result of breaking the law or as a penalty for not performing a duty. For example, loss of right to a SHARE because the shareholder, who has paid a deposit, has not fulfilled his or her undertaking to pay the balance when called upon to do so.

forint the standard monetary unit of Hungary, made up of 100 FILLER.

Fortune 500 the annual listing by *Fortune* magazine of the 500 largest manufacturers in the US.

forward exchange contract a contract to purchase FOREIGN EXCHANGE at a specified date in the future at an agreed exchange rate.

forward exchange rate the exchange rate agreed today for exchanging currency on a future date.

forward interest rate the INTEREST rate fixed today on a LOAN to be made on a future date.

forward market *same as* FUTURES MARKET.

forward rate agreement an agreement for a LOAN to take place on a future date but with an INTEREST rate fixed today.

forward trade a transaction that will be paid for at a future date but at a price agreed on the transaction date.

foul weather fund a STOCK that appears to perform well when the STOCK MARKET in general is performing badly.

Franc 1 the standard monetary unit of Andorra, Benin, Burkina-Faso, Burundi, Cameroon, the Central African Republic, Chad, Comoros, Congo, Côte d'Ivoire, Djibouti, Equatorial Guinea, Gabon, Guinea, Liechtenstein, Madagascar, Mali, Niger, Monaco, Rwanda, Senegal, Switzerland, Tahiti and Togo, made up of 100 CENTIMES. **2** the former standard monetary unit of Belgium, France and Luxembourg, replaced by the Euro on January 1 2002.

franchise a license granted to a manufacturer, distributor, trader, etc, that allows him or her to manufacture or sell a product or service in a particular area for a specified period of time. The grantor of the license (the **franchisor**) is usually paid a royalty on sales by the holder of the license (the **franchisee**).

fraud the acquiring of a financial advantage by means of deliberate deception or false representation.

Freddie Mac *See* FEDERAL HOME LOAN MORTGAGE CORPORATION.

free and clear a phrase meaning that something is owned completely, i.e. that there is no outstanding LOAN or MORTGAGE on it.

free capital 1 the SHARES in a public company that are available to members of the general public. **2** CAPITAL in the form of cash.

freehold property property that is legally held outright by a person or company.

free enterprise economy *or* **private enterprise economy** an economic system in which private individuals and companies, as opposed to the state, control the means of production and run and own businesses with the minimum of state interference.

free on board a term used to denote the basis on which an export contract has been made. By a free-on-board arrangement, the seller pays the cost of transporting the goods to the port of shipment and also the cost of loading them and any insurance charges payable up to that point. Thereafter the transport and insurance costs are the responsibility of the purchaser.

freeport a port that is free of IMPORT DUTIES or CUSTOMS DUTIES. Goods are usually imported by such ports when they are going to be subsequently re-exported. *See* ENTREPOT TRADE.

free trade the export and import of goods and services from one country to another without the imposition of restrictions such as TARIFFS or QUOTAS.

frictional unemployment the degree of unemployment that is considered to be consistent with the efficient running of an economy.

friendly hands a nickname for investors in an INITIAL PUBLIC OFFERING who intend to keep their holding for some time. They are not, therefore, looking for a quick, short-term PROFIT.

fringe benefits 1 any benefit given to an employee by his or her employer in addition to salary or wages. Such benefits include the use of a company car, expense accounts, cheap LOANS, private health plans and other benefits of a similar nature. Some of these benefits, such as a company car, are subject to tax. **2** benefits given by a company to its shareholders in addition to their dividends. Such benefits might include reductions in prices paid for the company's goods or Christmas gifts.

front money cash paid in advance as a down payment for something or to start a business.

frozen account a bank account from which no money can be withdrawn until the suspension is lifted by a court order.

frozen assets ASSETS that cannot be either used or realized.

functional budget a budget that has relevance to a particular function of a firm, such as production, marketing, etc.

funds flow statement a detailed account of all monies received and paid out during a specific accounting period.

fungibles 1 interchangeable securities, goods, etc, that allow for the replacement of one by another without any loss of value occurring. **2** perishable goods, the quantity of which can be estimated either by number or weight.

futures contract *or* **futures** an agreement to buy or sell a specified quantity of a fixed security, currency or commodity at a specified price at a specified date in the future.

futures market *or* **forward market** a market that deals in FUTURES CONTRACTS.

G

gainsharing a system of paying workers by which a proportion of pay is linked to gains in the level of productivity or to a reduction in the level of costs.

galloping inflation a term describing a period when the rate of INFLATION rises rapidly and by increasing amounts. The 1970s were a period of galloping inflation in the United States. See also HYPERINFLATION.

game theory a theory that when two or more people are in competition with each other, they will make their decisions in a rational and logical way.

Gantt chart developed by Henry L. Gantt, the Gantt chart is a bar chart used in production scheduling to compare actual performance with planned performance.

gap analysis a technique used in marketing that aims to establish the extent to which customers are satisfied by the products or services provided by a company. The gaps in the level of satisfaction can then be identified and any areas of dissatisfaction dealt with, either by improving a service or filling a demand by supplying a new service.

garnishment the withholding of all or part of an employee's earnings for the payment of a DEBT.

gatekeeper a person who is in charge of the flow of information in a large organization, often controlling both the information that goes into and leaves the organization and the information that is passed upwards and onwards in the organization structure.

GATT (General Agreement on Tariffs and Trade) an agreement signed in Geneva in 1947 intended to promote international trade by, for example, reducing import duties.

gazelle company a company that is growing extremely rapidly, as shown by its rising sales revenue.

gazumping a situation found mostly in house-buying in which the seller, having made an agreement to sell the house to a particular buyer, then sells it to another buyer for a higher price.

gazunder a situation whereby the potential buyer of a property suddenly lowers his or her bid at a very late stage in the negotiations, usually just before signing the papers.

GDP the abbreviated form of GROSS DOMESTIC PRODUCT.

gearing the ratio of a company's capital supplied by long-term funds having a fixed interest charge to its share capital. A company is said to have a low capital gearing when it raises most of its capital from issuing ORDINARY SHARES while a company is said to have a high capital gearing when most of its capital is from fixed-interest loans.

general accounting 1 includes all aspects of accounting as opposed to specializing in a single area such as tax **2** the department within an organization where all areas of accounting are practiced.

general cash offer an investment opportunity made to the public at large.

general mortgage bond a BOND that is secured by a mortgage against property owned by a company.

general partner a partner in an enterprise who, like the other participant(s), is personally responsible for all business DEBTS.

general partnership a PARTNERSHIP in which all the partners are GENERAL PARTNERS.

general price level (Brit) an index, such as the UK RETAIL PRICE INDEX, that gives an indication of the purchasing power of money.

generic brand a product sold at a lower price than a similar product that is protected by a TRADE-MARK.

generic name the general name used to identify a product or class of products, as opposed to the supplier's trade name or BRAND NAME that is used to identify a product. Thus personal organizer is a generic name but Filofax is a trade name and should thus be spelt with an initial capital letter. Likewise, vacuum cleaner is a generic name while Hoover is a trade name.

geodemographic segmentation a form of MARKET SEGMENTATION in which consumers are divided and categorized according to demographic variables such as income, age, marital status, etc, and are identified by geographical details such as zip codes.

ghosting in the STOCK MARKET, where two or more dealers collude to try and influence the market. This practice is illegal, but very difficult to detect and prove.

gifts inter vivos gifts that are made during the giver's lifetime as opposed to being bequeathed under the terms of the will of a deceased person. The treatment of such gifts is important for purposes of INHERITANCE TAX.

gilt-edged security (Brit) a fixed interest security or stock issued by the UK government as a means of borrowing money. Gilt-edged securities are considered to be a good investment because they carry an exceptionally low risk as the government is unlikely to default on their liabilities. The term is sometimes extended more generally to cover extremely low-risk securities.

Ginnie Mae *see* GOVERNMENT NATIONAL MORTGAGE ASSOCIATION.

glamor stock a STOCK MARKET expression for a heavily-traded STOCK whose price increases consistently.

glass ceiling the name given to the invisible barrier, usually created by discrimination, that prevents women and minorities from reaching posts in senior management in companies. This barrier continues, despite legislation designed to promote equal opportunities.

globalization or **internationalization** the investment in financial markets on an international basis.

glut the overproduction of a product or service resulting in a situation where the available products or service are so much in excess of market demand that they will not be bought at the current price.

GNP the abbreviated form of GROSS NATIONAL PRODUCT.

goal oriented a management strategy that establishes specific goals and formulates the methods by which these goals can be achieved.

godfather offer indicates an irresistible TAKEOVER BID; reference to the "Godfather" movies.

go-go stock a high-risk STOCK whose price rises very quickly – and often falls just as quickly.

going concern an enterprise that is trading steadily and profitably and will probably continue to do so.

going private a term describing the action taken by a public company, whose SHARES are bought and sold on the STOCK EXCHANGE, to buy back all its stock or arrange for its stock to be bought by an outside investor, in order to remove itself from the stock market. *See also* GOING PUBLIC.

going public a term describing the action take by a private company to offer its SHARES for sale to the public at large through the STOCK EXCHANGE. This is often done to raise money for investment in the business. *See also* GOING PRIVATE.

goldbrick shares in the STOCK MARKET, refers to SHARES in a stock that appear superficially to be valuable but are, in reality, almost worthless.

gold circle rate a rate of pay for a particular job that is higher than the maximum rate of pay established for that particular job.

golden handcuff a form of bonus payment offered to a key member of staff in a company to persuade him or her to stay rather than take his or her skills elsewhere.

golden handshake a form of severance payment offered to an employee as an inducement to him or her to leave the company or offered to an employee who is retiring from the company as a token of the company's gratitude for his or her service over the years.

golden hello a payment made as an inducement to a person to take up an employment offer with a company.

golden parachute a clause in the employment contract of a director or senior executive of a company that provides for generous severance payments if the director or executive is sacked or decides to leave the company in the event of a takeover.

golden share (Brit) a shareholding in a company that controls at least 51 per cent of the voting rights. This arrangement is adopted by the UK government as a means of interceding in the affairs of a company that has been privatized.

gold fixing the price of gold as decided on a daily basis by gold experts in Paris, London and Zurich. The price of gold has an influence on trading prices in all the major STOCK EXCHANGES.

goldilocks economy a phrase referring to the US economy in the late 1990s, and indicating that the prevailing economic situation was "just right".

gold standard a former monetary system in which the value of the standard unit of currency was by law made equal to a fixed weight of gold of a stated fineness.

good an economic product that is produced to satisfy a personal or business demand.

good faith having honest intentions. Business

transactions rely on the observance of reasonable and honest standards of behavior.

good 'til canceled order an order to buy or sell SHARES that remains in place until it is executed or canceled by either the investor or the BROKER.

goodwill a premium that the purchaser of a company must pay over and above the company's assets to allow for the company's reputation, trade contacts, brand names, management expertise, etc. Goodwill represents the difference between the value of the sum of its NET ASSETS and the total value of the business, perhaps as established by a stock market valuation.

goon (slang) a term describing a person hired to make trouble between management and workers. In the past, goons were used by management to interfere with workers' attempts to form unions; such practices are now illegal.

gopik *see* MANAT.

gorilla (slang) refers to a company that dominates a specific industry.

go-slow a form of INDUSTRIAL ACTION in which employees adopt a policy of deliberately working at a slow rate.

gourde *see* CENTIME.

Government National Mortgage Association (Ginnie Mae) a government organization concerned with the financing of federally guaranteed MORT-GAGES for home buyers.

government securities US Treasury SECURITIES that are negotiable.

government sponsored enterprises organizations that exist to help certain sectors of society, such as students, farmers and homeowners, borrow money at advantageous rates. For example, the Student Loan Marketing Association.

grace and notice provision a provision inserted in a LOAN agreement to avoid problems of seeming non-repayment caused by administrative error. It means that the borrower mentioned in the loan agreement will not automatically be held to be in DEFAULT if payment of INTEREST on repayment of CAPITAL is not made on the due date.

grain pit in the STOCK EXCHANGE, that area of the exchange where trading in agricultural COMMODITIES takes place. These include wheat, soybean and oat FUTURES.

grandfather clause a provision in a new law or rule that excludes those already engaged in the activity from complying with the new regulations.

grand strategy the method by which an enterprise expects to achieve its goals.

gray knight in a situation involving a company TAKEOVER BID, a potential bidder whose intentions are undeclared and thus unknown. *See* BLACK KNIGHT, WHITE KNIGHT, YELLOW KNIGHT.

graymail *see* GREENMAIL.

gray market 1 legal trading in goods of which there is a scarcity at a particular time. **2** a market in SHARES that have not been issued, although they are due to be issued within a short time.

Great Depression the period from late 1929 to the early 1940s in the United States when the economy slowed dramatically with a consequent rise in unemployment and its accompanying social problems and hardships. The Great Depression ended with the onset of World War II.

Greater Fool Theory the idea that, no matter how much someone has paid for something, there will always be someone else who will pay even more.

green audit a review of a company's business activities in terms of the environmental consequences of these activities. Such a review can identify, for example, sources of pollution or excessive use of a resource.

greenbacks US paper CURRENCY. The name is derived from the color of the ink used.

Green Card a permit issued by the US Immigration and Naturalization Service that allows non-US citizens to work in the USA. An employer who hires a foreign employee without a Green Card could be fined.

green currencies the currencies of members of the

EUROPEAN COMMUNITY using artificial rates of exchange for purposes of the Common Agricultural Policy. The object of green currencies is to protect farm prices in the member countries from the variations that might arise from fluctuations in rates of exchange.

greenfield project a business project or scheme that starts from scratch, specifically the building of a factory on a site in the country that has not been built on before.

greenmail *or* **graymail** a situation that can arise in a company TAKEOVER BID in which a large block of SHARES is purchased by a potential takeover bidder, who then sells the shares back to the directors of the company at a premium over the market price of the shares, the directors acting in this way to avert the bid.

grievance procedure the formal means by which an employee makes a complaint against his or her employer or union and by which that grievance can be resolved.

Groschen *see* SCHILLING.

gross domestic product (often abbreviated to **GDP**) the total monetary value of the goods and services produced by an economy over a specified period.

gross income 1 the income of a person or organization before the deduction of any allowable expenses that have been incurred in the earning of it. **2** income earned by a person or organization that is subject to tax but from which tax has not yet been deducted.

gross interest INTEREST earned before tax is paid.

gross margin *or* **gross profit** the difference between the sales revenue generated by a company and the cost of the products sold.

gross national product (often abbreviated to **GNP**) the total monetary value of all the goods and services produced in an economy over a specified period (GROSS DOMESTIC PRODUCT) plus the net income received from abroad in the form of interest, profits, rents and dividends.

gross profit *see* GROSS MARGIN.

gross receipts the total amount of money received before money is deducted to cover costs, taxation, etc.

gross sales the total amount of sales before deducting the total amount of returned goods.

groszy a monetary unit of Poland, one hundredth of a ZLOTY.

group dynamics the study of the interpersonal relationships between members of a department or other work group.

Group of Five (G5) consists of the United States, France, Germany, UK and Japan. These five leading economic countries meet periodically in an attempt to reach agreement on international economic problems.

Group of Seven (G7) the five members of the GROUP OF FIVE, plus Italy and Canada.

growth 1 increase in the value of an asset. **2** *same as* ECONOMIC GROWTH.

growth phase that period of time during which a company develops very quickly and rapidly increases its market share.

growth stock the STOCK of a company that has good prospects of overall future growth and at a rate higher than that expected for the average company.

guarani the standard monetary unit of Paraguay, made up of 100 CENTIMOS.

guarantee *same as* WARRANTY 1.

guarantor a person who guarantees to pay off a DEBT that has been incurred by someone else if that person should fail to repay the debt when it becomes due. See also ACCOMMODATION ENDORSEMENT.

guilder 1 the former standard monetary unit of the Netherlands, equal to 100 cents replaced by the Euro on January 1 2002. **2** the standard monetary unit of Surinam, equal to 100 cents. **3** the standard monetary unit of Antilles, equal to 100 cents.

gunslinger a term used to describe a PORTFOLIO MANAGER who concentrates on very high-risk, high-return investments.

H

halala a monetary unit of Saudi Arabia, equal to one hundredth of a RIYAL.

haler a monetary unit of the Czech Republic and Slovakia, equal to one hundredth of a koruna.

halo effect *see* HORNS AND HALO EFFECT.

hand-to-mouth buying purchasing only small amounts as and when the need arises. When a company is experiencing financial difficulties, it may resort to hand-to-mouth buying to conserve as much cash as possible.

hao a monetary unit of Vietnam, equal to one tenth of a dong.

hard currency a currency that is commonly accepted throughout the world and so is valued because of its universal purchasing power. It is, therefore, in strong demand.

hard sell the use of a very forceful approach to selling.

hardware the electronic and mechanical parts that make up a computer system. These include the disk drive, the central processing unit, the keyboard, the visual display unit and the printer.

harvesting strategy a business strategy in which profits are maximized at the expense of reinvestment.

headhunter an expression describing a person or company that specializes in finding people to fill key management, technical or professional vacancies. These vacancies are not, normally, advertised in the usual way. The headhunter targets a likely candidate and tries to persuade him or her to leave their current employer and work for the company that has hired the headhunter to fill the vacancy.

health maintenance organization (HMO) a group health insurance scheme in which members agree to use the doctors and hospitals that have agreed to take part in the scheme. The members then enjoy lower healthcare costs. HMOs also encourage preventive medicine and encourage members to take care of their health on a day-to-day basis.

hedging the act of decreasing the degree of uncertainty about future price movements in commodities, securities and foreign currency. Hedging can take the form of carrying out purchases in the FUTURES MARKET or taking out an OPTION that restricts the option-holder's exposure to price variations.

hedging against inflation an attempt to protect one's CAPITAL against depreciation by INFLATION by purchasing EQUITIES or making other investments that are likely to rise in value as the general level of prices rises.

hemline theory the rather fanciful idea that STOCK prices move in the same direction as women's hemlines. It is based on the notion that hemlines move up and down according to fluctuating levels of confidence and optimism in society in general.

hidden reserve funds that are held in reserve by a company but do not appear on the balance sheet. These funds occur when the ASSETS of a company are undervalued or when its LIABILITIES are overvalued.

high grade bond a very high quality BOND. It may offer a lower INTEREST rate than other bonds but it tends to be more secure.

high-yield bond *see* JUNK BOND.

hire purchase a method of buying goods on an installment basis in which a DEPOSIT is paid to secure possession of the goods and then a fixed number of installments is paid until ownership is secured.

historical cost a system of valuing units of stock or other assets by basing it on the original cost to the company.

historical cost accounting a system of accounting based mainly on the original costs involved in transactions.

hit the bricks (slang) an expression meaning that maximum effort will have to be made to achieve a specific objective in a specific time.

holdback in business, usually means money that is not paid until certain conditions are complied with. For example, the withholding of payment for goods until they are received, inspected and found to be satisfactory.

holding company (Brit) in the UK, a company that holds shares in other companies, usually its subsidiaries, the shareholding being either 100 per cent or more than 50 per cent of the total.

home banking the carrying out of routine bank transactions by a bank customer by means of a home computer linked to the relevant bank's computer.

homeworking work that is performed in the worker's own home premises, often on a freelance basis.

honor in business, to accept and fulfill an obligation such as in a CONTRACT, or to pay when due, as for a DEBT.

honorarium a payment to someone for a service for which there is no legal obligation to pay, such as giving an honorarium to a speaker at a conference.

Hoover Commission created in 1947 by Herbert C. Hoover, this Federal commission was charged with reorganizing the executive branch of the government and improving its efficiency.

horizontal acquisition a MERGER between two or more competitors.

horizontal marketing a marketing system in which two or more companies in the same industry and at the same level join forces and resources to exploit a marketing opportunity, for example in a global market.

horns and halo effect an effect that creates an unusually good or bad impression of an employee on an employer. Such an effect may lead to gross misjudgment, leading to efficient employees with the 'horns effect' failing to gain promotion or even failing to get a job in the first place, or leading to extremely inefficient people being appointed to posts for which they are unsuited or to their being promoted beyond their powers.

hot money CAPITAL that is moved quickly from one country to another according to INTEREST or exchange rate changes.

human asset accounting the idea that the employees of a firm, at every level, are that firm's main ASSET and this should be accounted for on the firm's BALANCE SHEET.

human resource management the management of people so as to achieve a maximum individual performance from each worker that will add to the general overall effectiveness of a company. Workers are encouraged to establish personal goals and rewards and to adjust their behavior in line with the objectives of the company for which they work. Emphasis is placed on the achieving of job satisfaction by workers and on their general morale and well being, this being seen as vital to the efficiency and well being of the company.

hush money (slang) an expression used to describe a payment of money to someone, as a bribe, to make sure that person keeps silent about something.

hypothecation authorization that is given to a banker to enable him or her to sell goods that have been pledged as security for a LOAN if payments on the loan have not been kept up.

hyperinflation an extremely high rate of INFLATION.

I

IBRD *see* WORLD BANK.

ICC *see* INTERSTATE COMMERCE COMMISSION.

ideal capacity the maximum possible output of a machine in ideal conditions.

idle money money that is not invested and therefore not earning any INTEREST.

idle time the time during which a piece of equipment or an operator is not productive.

illiquid 1 not having enough funds to meet current obligations. If this situation cannot be resolved fairly quickly, a company may be forced to become bankrupt. *See* BANKRUPTCY. **2** a word used to describe any ASSET that cannot easily be converted into CASH.

image in marketing, the way in which a product or service is seen by those in its target market or by the public in general.

IMF *see* INTERNATIONAL MONETARY FUND.

IMM *see* INTERNATIONAL MONETARY MARKET.

immediate settlement concluding a SHARE purchase within five business days.

impact day the day on which the terms of a new SHARE ISSUE is announced.

impeachment the means by which an elected official can be removed from office, usually for committing a crime or for misconduct.

implied contract an agreement that is not written down, but can be reasonably inferred under the circumstances.

implied policy a policy that is not written down, but can be interpreted from the actions or behavior of the people involved. For example, male employees of a company may be expected to wear conservative neckties to work; this is not written into their contracts but is a customary practice from which they are not expected to deviate.

implied terms the conditions of a CONTRACT, such as a contract of employment, that are not explicitly stated but are implicit, for example because the conditions are part of common law.

import deposit a sum of money that is paid by an importer to the relevant government when goods arrive in a country prior to their sale. These import deposits are used to discourage imports with a view to protecting a government's BALANCE OF PAYMENTS.

import duty a tax that is levied by a government on imported products. Import duty is an important method of raising revenue for the government and is also used as a barrier to foreign competition against domestic products.

imports goods or services that are purchased from another country.

import surcharge an extra tax that is imposed by a government on certain imports in addition to the usual IMPORT DUTY.

impound legally to seize property, funds and so on to hold as security for a DEBT.

imprest a system used in the control of PETTY CASH expenditure in which a certain sum of money is made available at the beginning of an accounting period as an opening balance, also called imprest. At the end of the accounting period vouchers are collected in respect of any money spent and the balance or float restored to the original amount. The system is intended to limit losses from fraud.

impulse buying the purchase of a product by a consumer on impulse rather than because of planned intention.

imputed cost a cost that is not actually incurred by a company but that is allowed for in management accounting records so that the costs that are incurred by operations that are not similar in all respects can be compared. For example, a cost for rent might be introduced in the management accounting records of a firm that does not pay rent so that costs may be compared with those of a firm that does have to pay rent.

in-and-out in the STOCK MARKET, buying and

selling SHARES within a very short time, possibly on the same day.

Inc. *see* INCORPORATED.

income money received in recompense for work done, as a return on investment, by way of rent received when renting out property, etc.

income and expenditure account an account that records the income and expenditure of an organization, such as a charity, whose main purpose is not the generation of profit. The account is similar to a PROFIT AND LOSS ACCOUNT and results in either an excess of income over expenditure or vice versa.

income bond a BOND paying INTEREST only if it is earned by the organization which has issued the bond. Income bonds are often issued during the reorganization of an unsuccessful enterprise.

income smoothing the process undertaken by some companies of manipulating some items in their financial statements. This is a form of CREATIVE ACCOUNTING and is carried out in order to avoid wide variations in profit from one accounting period to another and in order to achieve a smooth, steady and increasing pattern of profit over the years.

income statement a financial statement that summarizes all revenues and expenses of an enterprise over a specific period.

income tax a form of TAX that is imposed by the government on income, such as wages, interest, rents, etc. It is usually imposed on a sliding scale so that people who earn more pay higher rates of tax, there being some predetermined upper limit.

income tax allowance (Brit) an allowance that is deducted from a tax payer's GROSS INCOME before the calculation of his or her INCOME TAX liability. In the UK everyone receives a personal allowance, certain categories of people, such as single parents and older people, receiving higher personal allowances than others.

incorporated, Inc. a designation indicating that the owners of a business have LIMITED LIABILITY for the firm's DEBTS. *See also* GENERAL PARTNERSHIP.

increasing capital an increase in the number of SHARES or in the value of shares in a company in order to augment the amount of its authorized SHARE CAPITAL.

indemnity an agreement by which one party undertakes to compensate another party for losses sustained. For example, an insurance company enters into an indemnity arrangement with a client for losses sustained as a result of theft, loss, damage, etc, to the client's property.

indenture a written agreement between all parties involved which specifies reciprocal duties and rights. For example, the CONTRACT between bondholders and the issuing organization is an indenture.

index-linked the term used to describe economic variables such as wages, benefits, etc, when these are related to a price index in some predetermined way.

indicated staff the theoretical number of people required to perform a particular task at STANDARD RATE.

indirect costs costs that cannot be ascribed directly to a particular product or cost unit and thus are regarded as OVERHEADS.

indirect labor the part of a work force that is not directly involved in the manufacture of products or the provision of services. The indirect labor force includes clerical staff, cleaning staff, etc.

indirect labor budget in manufacturing, an estimate of the LABOR COSTS not directly associated with the manufacture of a product. Such costs might include wages for janitors, security guards etc.

indirect materials materials that are not actually incorporated in a product but are a necessary part of the production process. Such materials include lubricants and cleaning materials.

indirect quote the number of units of a foreign currency needed to buy one US dollar.

indirect tax (Brit) a form of tax that is designed to be borne by people or organizations other than those who pay the tax to the government. For example, in the UK value-added tax (VAT) is a form of indirect tax. VAT is paid to the government by traders on goods and services but the cost is ultimately borne by the consumer of the goods or services.

individual proprietorship *see* SOLE PROPRIETORSHIP.

Individual Retirement Account (IRA) an arrangement whereby an employee may set aside part of their earnings for their retirement. The money is invested in STOCKS, SHARES, certificates of deposit and so forth.

industrial action organized action that is undertaken by employees in order to bring pressure to bear on employers to get them to agree to their demands relating to level of wages, working conditions, terms of employment, etc. It usually forms part of an INDUSTRIAL DISPUTE. There are various forms of industrial action, such as WORK-TO-RULE, GO-SLOW and STRIKE. Industrial action is sometimes official and has the backing of the relevant LABOR UNION or unions and is sometimes unofficial.

industrial advertising advertising directed to other businesses, such as the sale of raw materials or services needed for the production of other goods or services. Industrial advertising is mainly restricted to trade publications.

industrial consumer a purchaser of goods and services for use in other business enterprises, such as manufacturing firms, retail outlets and financial organizations.

industrial democracy a system in which workers participate in some way in the management of an organization and/or share in its profits. Industrial democracies can take various forms. Some organizations have workers' councils, which have a voice in decision making, and some appoint a member of the workforce to the board of directors. In the case of an organization that is a WORKERS' COOPERATIVE, the policies are formulated or sanctioned by the workforce.

industrial discipline codes of practice put in place by an employer that set out rules and regulations, and the means by which these will be enforced.

industrial dispute a dispute between employees and employers, usually arising because of dissatisfaction over pay, working conditions, terms of employment, discipline, etc, and often involving INDUSTRIAL ACTION.

industrial espionage the act of spying illegally on the activities of a competitor in order to gain information about new products, sales strategy, etc.

industrial hygiene 1 a specialist medical field concerned with the study of the causes, effects and prevention of industrial diseases and the promotion of workers' health and well being. **2** those factors in the industrial environment that affect the health and well being of workers.

Industrial psychology the study of human behavior in the workplace. Industrial psychology examines areas such as selection, testing, interviewing, training and performance.

industrial relations the relationship between workers and management, including the relationship between LABOR UNIONS and management.

Industrial Revolution the generally accepted name given to that period of great change in economic and social organization from about 1750 to 1850. It began in Britain, spread to Europe in the early 19ᵗʰ century and to the United States from about 1860. Its most notable feature was the change from a land and agriculture-based economy to a factory economy, facilitated by the invention of such machines as the steam engine. Road, railroad and canal building transformed transportation and new overseas markets opened up. Huge cities were built as workers moved from the land to the factories, and the period also saw the rise of the labor unions and political agitation.

industrial union a LABOR UNION that includes all types of workers in a given industry, such as the United Automobile Workers.

industrial waste emissions, effluents, unwanted materials and other items resulting from manufacturing or other operations such as processing. The safe disposal of industrial waste is of paramount importance. *See* ENVIRONMENTAL PROTECTION AGENCY, SOCIAL RESPONSIBILITY.

industry 1 the branch of commercial enterprise that is concerned with the manufacture of goods, as in heavy industry. **2** a branch of commercial enterprise that is concerned with the creation of related goods or services, as in the soft drinks industry.

industry-wide bargaining when a LABOR UNION or a group of unions negotiate an agreement with an employer or employers within a given industry.

inelastic demand when the demand for a product tends to stay the same even if the price rises or falls. The demand for bread, for example, is likely to stay the same whether the price rises or falls.

inertia selling a form of selling in which goods are sent to people who have not ordered them in the hope that they will keep the goods and pay for them and not send them back.

inflation an increase in the general level of prices in an economy with a resultant fall in the purchasing power of money. Inflation has a particularly disadvantageous effect on people on fixed incomes as well as having a bad effect generally on the economy.

inflation accounting an accounting system that aims to take account of INFLATION and so arrive at a statement of the true profitability of a company, unlike historic cost accounting.

inflation-escalator clause a clause in a CONTRACT which takes account of possible future increases or decreases in INFLATION which could affect, for example, production and labor costs.

inflation risk the risk that rising INFLATION will affect the real value of the RETURN an investor will receive on his or her investment.

infrastructure a country's essential system of communications, transportation, utilities etc.

inherent delay in a production operation, the period when a worker is idle because of circumstances outside his or her control, such as waiting for the machine to complete a process.

inherent skill the ability to do something without training.

inheritance tax 1 a graduated tax imposed by any state in the US on the estates of deceased persons **2 (Brit)** a form of WEALTH TAX that is payable on a proportion of assets when these are transferred to beneficiaries, a certain amount of the assets being tax-free. In the UK assets that are transferred to beneficiaries more than seven years before the death of the transferor and assets that are transferred between three and seven years are subject to a lower rate of tax.

initial public offering (IPO) a company's first public sale of STOCK. IPOs are usually issued by new, small companies and investors must be prepared to accept high levels of risk, but also with the possibility of making large profits.

injunction a court order to an organization or a person prohibiting a certain course of action

Inland Revenue (Brit) the UK government department that is responsible for the assessing of the taxation liabilities of individuals and organizations and for the collection of money owed in taxation.

innkeeper's lien the right of a hotel or motel operator to keep the baggage of a resident as security for payment of goods supplied and/or services rendered. *See also* LIEN, CARRIER'S LIEN, MECHANIC'S LIEN.

insiders company directors and senior officials who have access to confidential information about the company's performance and prospects. *See also* INSIDER DEALING.

insider dealing the dealing in FINANCIAL SECURITIES by someone who has access to information that is not yet generally available and would affect the price of the securities, the aim being to exploit this knowledge to make a profit or avoid a loss. Company directors, employees and financial advisers and others in a position to obtain such information are prohibited from taking part in insider dealing.

insolvency the inability to meet one's DEBTS when these become due. This may lead to BANKRUPTCY in the case of individuals or to LIQUIDATION in the case of companies.

institutional investors very large organizations, such as INSURANCE COMPANIES and pension funds, that have large amounts of money to invest and therefore exert considerable influence on the STOCK MARKET.

institutional lender a financial organization, such as a COMMERCIAL BANK, that makes LOANS or INVESTMENTS on behalf of its customers or depositors.

instrument a formal legal document.

insurance a system that provides a person or company with protection against financial loss that may result from damage to or theft of property, loss of property or against death or injury in return for the payment of an INSURANCE PREMIUM. The person or company provided with this protection is known as the **insured** and the company that provides it is known as the **insurer**, often an INSURANCE COMPANY.

insurance broker a person or firm acting as an intermediary in bringing together clients seeking insurance cover and companies specializing in providing this cover, the broker usually being paid commission on the sale by the relevant INSURANCE COMPANY.

insurance company a financial institution that underwrites the risk of financial loss as a result of damage to or theft of property or loss of property or the risk of death or injury. *See* INSURANCE.

insurance policy a document that formally states the terms of an insurance contract between the insurer and the insured person or company.

insurance premium a sum of money paid either once or in regular installments to a company providing insurance against damage, theft or loss of property or against death or injury.

insured mail mail sent through the US Postal Service that is protected from loss or damage by INSURANCE.

intangible asset an asset that cannot be touched or seen. The GOODWILL of a business is an example, as is COPYRIGHT.

integrated accounts company accounting records that are kept in one set of books so that the FINANCIAL ACCOUNTS and the COST ACCOUNTS are together in an integrated form.

intellectual property the legal ownership of certain INTANGIBLE ASSETS, such as COPYRIGHT, TRADEMARKS or PATENT.

intensive distribution a distribution strategy that is aimed at obtaining the maximum possible number of outlets for a product or products.

interbank market the section of the London money market in which banks lend to each other and to other large financial institutions.

intercompany loan a LOAN made by one sector of an organization to another sector of the same organization.

interest the charge that is made for borrowing money in the form of a loan. Interest charges may be fixed or variable and are paid on a regular basis. Interest may take the form of **compound interest** or **simple interest**. Simple interest is based only on the original amount of the loan. Compound interest is based on the original amount of the loan plus the previously accumulated interest.

interest rate the amount that a borrower is required to pay for a LOAN, usually expressed as a percentage of the sum borrowed.

interim dividend a DIVIDEND that is paid to SHAREHOLDERS midway through a FISCAL YEAR.

interim report a company financial statement that is issued for a period of less than a FISCAL YEAR, often half-yearly. These are often sent to SHAREHOLDERS to keep them up to date with the progress of the company.

intermediation the role of a bank or other financial

institution in acting as an intermediary between two parties in a business transaction, for example, between a borrower and a lender in a LOAN transaction.

internal audit an AUDIT that is carried out in a company by members of its own staff, rather than by EXTERNAL AUDITORS, so as to ascertain that the company's internal control system is operating effectively and that there are no incidences of theft or fraud. Internal audits may deal with issues other than financial ones, such as the monitoring of the carrying out of equal opportunities legislation.

internal growth a method of business growth in a company that is self-generated, in that the growth is a result of the exploitation of the company's resources, such as market development and extension or new-product development.

internal growth rate the rate at which a firm can expand without borrowing money from outside sources. A company's internal growth rate is supported by its PROFITS.

Internal Revenue Code the tax rules that are administered by the INTERNAL REVENUE SERVICE.

Internal Revenue Service (IRS) a US government department responsible for the administration of INCOME TAX laws and the collection of income taxes. The IRS is part of the US Department of the Treasury.

International Bank for Reconstruction and Development (IBRD) *see* WORLD BANK.

international corporation a corporation active in two or more countries.

internationalization *see* GLOBALIZATION.

International Monetary Fund (IMF) headquartered in Washington, D.C., the IMF was founded in 1944 as an agency of the United Nations. Its purpose is to encourage monetary cooperation between countries and promote international trade.

International Monetary Market (IMM) a department of the Chicago Mercantile Exchange, established in 1972. It trades in FUTURES in US TREASURY BILLS, foreign currency, EURODOLLARS etc.

interstate commerce business conducted between organizations in two or more states. Such business activities are regulated by the Federal government. See also INTERSTATE COMMERCE COMMISSION.

Interstate Commerce Commission (ICC) Established in 1887, this federal agency enforces the Interstate Commerce Act of 1887, which regulates the transportation industry between states. Its areas of jurisdiction include railroad, water and motor services.

intestate (of a person) dying without having made a valid will.

in the black a phrase meaning than an account is in profit or has a credit balance.

in the penalty box a phrase indicating that a company's SHARE price has fallen to a lower than usual level. The company is therefore "in the penalty box."

in the red a phrase meaning than an account is overdrawn or has a DEBIT balance.

Intrastate commerce a business activity carried on solely within the boundaries of a particular state. Such a business is not subject to the rules of the Interstate Commerce Act of 1887. *See also* INTERSTATE COMMERCE.

introduction a method of raising new share capital by issuing company shares at an agreed price to MARKET MAKERS and STOCKBROKERS rather than directly to the public. It is usually employed by established companies as a means of raising new capital at a relatively low administrative cost.

inventory a list of all the tangible ASSETS owned by a person or an organization.

inventory investment investment in raw materials, WORK IN PROGRESS and finished stock.

inventory valuation the valuation of raw materials, WORK IN PROGRESS and finished stock.

investment a financial expenditure made in order to acquire an income-producing property.

investment bank a financial organization that buys

new BOND or STOCK issues in their entirety then sells them on in smaller amounts to other dealers and the public. The investment bank, therefore, takes on the risk for the success of the new ISSUE.

investment climate the overall economic situation in the financial markets.

investment grant a grant that is made to a company by a government as an incentive to investment in plant, machinery, buildings, etc, as a means of encouraging new investment in an area.

investment income a person's income that is derived from investments rather than from employment.

investment manager the person who is responsible for a PORTFOLIO of INVESTMENTS. An investment manager may be self-employed or may work for an investment company.

investment trust company a LIMITED COMPANY that invests its shareholders' funds in a variety of financial securities, the shares being bought and sold on the stock market.

investor an individual or organization that owns a financial ASSET.

investor relations the means through which an organization communicates with its INVESTORS.

invisible assets *same as* INTANGIBLE ASSETS.

invisible earnings the earnings from abroad that

contribute to a country's balance of payments as a result of transactions involving the sale of services relating to tourism, banking, insurance, etc, rather than to the sale of goods.

invisible hand the idea, put forward by the Scottish philosopher and economist, Adam Smith, in his book "The Wealth of Nations" (1776), that there is an unseen force that guides society through enlightened self-interest. The welfare of society, he suggested, is assured when all the people who make up that society act in their own self-interest.

invitation for bid an invitation from a commercial or government organization inviting suppliers to submit price quotations on specific products or services.

invoice a document that shows the amount that is due to the issuer of the invoice for goods or services supplied, itemizes the products and individual prices and is issued as a request for payment.

IOU "I owe you." An informal acceptance of a CASH DEBT.

IPO *see* INITIAL PUBLIC OFFERING.

IRA *see* INDIVIDUAL RETIREMENT ACCOUNT.

IRS *see* INTERNAL REVENUE SERVICE.

issue the number of shares or the amount of stock that is on offer to the public at a particular time.

issued share a share that has been assigned by the directors of a company to an applicant and paid for in full.

issued share capital the amount of the authorized SHARE CAPITAL for which shareholders have subscribed.

issue price the price at which a new issue of shares is issued to the public.

issuer a legal entity, such as a corporation or a government, that is empowered to issue a SECURITY.

issuing house a financial house, such as a merchant bank, that arranges the issue of new STOCKS and shares for companies and organizes the flotation of private companies in the STOCK EXCHANGE.

J

jiao a monetary unit of China, equal to one tenth of a YUAN.

JIT the abbreviated form of JUST IN TIME.

job an identifiable piece of work or unit of service carried out by a company.

job analysis a research process involving the detailed analysis of a particular JOB, involving such things as the nature of the tasks involved in the job, the qualifications of the people involved in it, the equipment required to carry it out and its relationship to other jobs carried out by the company.

jobber 1 a wholesaler who buys goods (job lots) from manufacturers, importers or other wholesalers and sells them on to retailers. **2** in manufacturing, a company that produces goods to order *See* JOB ORDER PRODUCTION.

jobbing 1 the work of a JOBBER. **2** a production process by which small numbers of a product are produced for individual customers.

job description a detailed statement of the tasks and responsibilities that an employee is expected by the employer to carry out as part of his or her employment.

job design the process of putting together the

various elements that go together to form JOBS.

job number a number that is assigned to a JOB so that any costs attached to it may be assigned to that number and so eventually be allowed for in the overall costs of the job.

job order production the manufacturing of a set quantity of a particular item for a specific customer. Job order production is the opposite of MASS PRODUCTION.

job satisfaction the sense of satisfaction and fulfillment experienced by people as a result of their work. It is in the interests of employers as well as employees to try to achieve a high level of job satisfaction in the workplace, as it is generally accepted that workers who have a high level of job satisfaction work more efficiently, have fewer accidents and have a better attendance record than workers with a low level of job satisfaction.

job security the degree of certainty of continued employment with a particular company experienced by workers. It is low in cases where the company is seen to be sustaining losses or is intent on achieving a greater profit ratio and workers fear the prospect of redundancy. The tendency in the 1980s and 1990s for employers to issue short-term contracts or stated-term contracts, sometimes renewable at the end of the stated period, reduced levels of job security.

job-sharing the division of the work of one full-time employee between two or more part-time employees, each part-time worker being paid on a pro rata basis according to the number of hours worked. The advantages to employees are obvious in that job-sharing allows people who may be able to work only a limited number of hours a greater choice of work, and usually more interesting work, but the system can be disadvantageous to employers because of increased employment costs.

joint account a bank account that is held in the names of two or more people.

joint and several liability LIABILITY for a DEBT that is undertaken by a group. If any member of the group fails to meet his or her liability, the rest of the group will share the whole of the liability.

joint rate setting where wage rates are set through negotiation between management and union, rather than imposed by management alone.

joint-stock company a form of company in which a group of people supply funds with which to finance a business, receiving in return a number of shares in the company.

joint venture a business venture entered into by two, or sometimes more, parties. Two companies might be engaged in a joint venture and yet still function also as independent, separate companies. Unlike a PARTNERSHIP, a joint venture is set up for a particular activity and sometimes for a particular period of time. It enables companies, for example, to share complementary resources and skills, to share costs and to gain access to new markets.

judgment lien a court order that allows a CREDITOR to lay claim to a property in order to satisfy an unpaid DEBT. See also CARRIER'S LIEN, INNKEEPER'S LIEN, MECHANIC'S LIEN.

Jumbo loan LOANS of $1 billion or more.

junior debt in a BANKRUPTCY, the holders of junior DEBT may make a claim on the firm's ASSETS only after the holders of SENIOR DEBT have been paid.

junk bond a high-interest, high-risk BOND issued as a means of financing a TAKEOVER BID.

just in time (often abbreviated to **JIT**) a manufacturing system in which materials, components and products are not produced for or delivered to the next production stage or to the customer until the exact time at which they are needed. The system aims at synchronizing the flow of materials between production stages and so keep to a minimum the amount of stock relating to work-in-progress. It also aims to reduce the amount of finished product stored by the company by timing the final assembly of products to match the rate of customers' orders. Thus both stockholding costs and space requirements can be reduced, but the disadvantages of the system are that production is more likely to be held up by delivery hold-ups of materials or components.

K

Kaffirs (Brit) the informal name given to South African gold-mining shares on the London Stock Exchange.

Kangaroos (Brit) the informal name given to Australian shares on the London Stock Exchange, particularly those concerned with mining, tobacco and land.

khoum a monetary unit of Mauritania, equal to one fifth of an OUGUIYA.

kickback a payment made to a person or organization as a reward for their help or influence in a particular project. Giving kickbacks for favors is generally considered an unethical practice in the United States.

kicked upstairs (slang) an expression used of someone who has been promoted to a higher position in a firm, usually an executive post.

kicking the tires a slang phrase that describes the research undertaken by prospective investors into the company they are considering investing in. It is taken from the practice of literally kicking the tires when looking at cars on a used car lot.

killer bees investment bankers who assist companies looking for a hostile takeover opportunity.

kina the standard monetary unit of Papua New Guinea, made up of 100 TOEA.

kip the standard monetary unit of Laos, made up of 100 at.

kite an informal name for ACCOMMODATION BILL.

kiting (slang) in finance, to write and deposit CHECKS on accounts at two or more banks to take advantage of the float, or time taken to process the checks, thus giving the impression that there is more money than there actually is. Kiting is considered to be a fraudulent practice.

knock-for-knock agreement an agreement between motor insurance companies by which they pay for any accident damage sustained by their own policy-holders, irrespective of who was to blame for the accident.

kobo a monetary unit of Nigeria, equal to one hundredth of a NAIRA.

kopeck *see* ROUBLE.

koruna *see* HALER.

krona 1 the standard monetary unit of Sweden, made up 100 ore. **2** the standard monetary unit of Iceland, made up of 100 EYRIR.

krone 1 the standard monetary unit of Denmark, made up of 100 ore. **2** the standard monetary unit of Norway, made up of 100 ore. **3** the standard monetary unit of Greenland, made up of 100 ore. **4** the standard monetary unit of the Faeroe Islands, made up of 100 ore.

kroon the standard monetary unit of Estonia before 1940.

Krugerrand a South African coin that contains one troy ounce of gold. It is used by investors to get round restrictions imposed on the holding of gold.

kuna the standard monetary unit of Croatia, made up of 100 lipas.

kuru a monetary unit of Turkey, equal to one hundredth of a LIRA.

kwacha 1 the standard monetary unit of Malawi, made up of 100 TAMBALA. **2** the standard monetary unit of Zambia, made up of 100 NGWEE.

kwanza the standard monetary unit of Angola, made up of 100 LWEI.

kyat the standard monetary unit of Myanmar (Burma), made up of 100 PYAS.

L

laari a monetary unit of the Maldives that is worth one hundredth of a RUFIYAA.

labeling laws Federal and state laws that require safe packaging and warning labels on containers of hazardous materials.

labor costs the cost of the wages paid to workers who are concerned with the manufacture of a product or the carrying out of a service.

labor force 1 the total number of people who are employed by a firm in the manufacture of goods or the carrying out of services. **2** the total number of people who are available to produce goods and carry out services.

labor force participation rate the percentage of the total LABOR FORCE that is working or looking for work.

labor grade the category or level applied to a job, usually based on such criteria as skill, experience and education. Manufacturing production jobs, for example, will have different labor grades according to the skills needed to perform different tasks.

labor-intensive the term used to refer to an industry or firm that employs a relatively high number of people and in which the LABOR COSTS are thus high, particularly in proportion to the cost of raw materials or capital equipment.

labor law the body of legislation concerned with INDUSTRIAL RELATIONS and employment.

Labor-Management Reporting and Disclosure Act of 1959, Landrum-Griffin Act of 1959 Federal labor relations acts which regulate the internal affairs of unions and union officials and control picketing with the aim of eliminating racketeering and corruption.

labor relations *same as* INDUSTRIAL RELATIONS.

labor turnover rate the proportion of the number of employees who leave a firm, organization or industry in a stated period in relation to the average number of employees working in the firm or industry during that period.

labor union an organization of workers, the aim of which is to protect the interests of its members and to negotiate pay and conditions of employment with employers.

Lady Godiva Accounting Principles (LGAP) a phrase first used after the Enron scandal and referring to an accounting theory that insists on full and complete disclosure of all relevant information.

Lady Macbeth Strategy in a hostile TAKEOVER BID situation, where an apparently neutral third party, a WHITE KNIGHT, enters the negotiations with a more acceptable offer, but later joins with the party making the unwelcome bid, the

BLACK KNIGHT. The phrase is taken from Shake-speare's play "Macbeth" and is a reference to the manipulative and cunning Lady Macbeth.

lagging *see* LEADING AND LAGGING.

laissez-faire an economic philosophy that advocates a free-market system over a state-regulated system and recommends keeping government intervention to a minimum.

lakh in India, Pakistan and Bangladesh the word used to refer to 100,000 RUPEES as well as meaning simply 100,000 of anything.

lame duck an informal term used to describe a company that is experiencing trading problems and sustaining losses to the extent that its survival may be threatened. The term is used particularly of failing companies that, for some reason, are strategically important to the government and to which the government might then therefore offer support.

LAN the abbreviated form of LOCAL AREA NETWORK.

laptop computer a small personal computer that can be battery-operated and has a flat display screen that folds over the keyboard when not in use for ease of portability.

lari the standard monetary unit of Georgia.

lats the standard monetary unit of Latvia, which is made up of 100 santims.

laundering an informal term used to describe the processing of money acquired by some illegal means in such a way that the money appears to have come from a legal source.

lay-off the termination of an employee's employment, either temporarily or permanently, usually because of a reduced demand for the work or services in the production of which he or she is involved.

leading and lagging methods used at the end of a company's financial year to improve the cash position. Leading refers to the arrangement of the acceleration of the settlement of outstanding financial obligations and lagging refers to the delaying of these.

lead time the time intervening between the placing of an order and the goods being received.

leakage in the STOCK MARKET, the release of sensitive information to certain people or organizations before a formal public announcement.

LEAPS acronym for Long-term Equity Anticipation Securities. These are a type of long-term OPTION.

learning curve the process by which the labor force and management of a company gain experience in a new technology or new production process from cumulative contact and so become more efficient and cost-effective. This enables the unit cost of production to be reduced.

lease a legal contract between the owner (**lessor**)

of an ASSET to a person or company (**lessee**) by which the lessee has the right to use the asset for a specified length of time at an agreed rental fee, the lessor continuing to be the legal owner.

leaseback an arrangement by which an ASSET is sold to another person or company on condition that the asset is then leased back or rented to the original owner for a specified period of time at an agreed rental fee. The system is usually used as a means of raising finance.

leasing the hiring of an ASSET, such as a vehicle or piece of equipment, by one firm from another rather than purchasing it. This avoids the capital cost of owning the asset, leaving the capital to be used for business operations and is considered advantageous in the case of equipment that is likely to become obsolete quite quickly.

ledger a collection of company accounting records of a similar type, such as the PURCHASE, or creditors', LEDGER or the SALES, or debtors', LEDGER. Originally ledgers consisted of large books in which entries were recorded in handwriting but now they often take the form of computer records.

ledger cash an organization's cash balance as indicated in its financial statements.

legacy a gift of personal property given by someone through his or her will. It may include money, real estate, furniture, jewelry and so forth.

legal bankruptcy the legal means through which an organization is liquidated. See LIQUIDATION.

legal capital the value of a company's SHARES as recorded in its financial statements.

legal entity a person or organization, such as a PARTNERSHIP or corporation, that is able to own property or enter a transaction and may be sued for failure to adhere to the terms of that transaction.

legal reserve the minimum amount of money that such financial entities as insurance companies, etc, must hold by law as security in the interests of their customers.

legal tender money that, by law, is acceptable in discharge of public or private DEBTS, unless the relevant contract requires payment in a specific kind of money.

lek the standard monetary unit of Albania, being made up of 100 qindar.

legatee a person who receives a gift of personal property through a will. *See* LEGACY.

legator a person who bequeaths personal property through a will. *See* LEGACY.

lempira the standard monetary unit of Honduras, being made up of 100 CENTAVOS.

lend in finance, to provide money to a person or organization on a temporary basis, with the expectation that it will be returned in its entirety and usually with INTEREST added.

lender an individual or organization that makes a business out of providing funds for others for a fee.

lender of last resort the central bank of a country, which is in control of its banking system. In the US this is the Federal Reserve System and in the UK, it is the Bank of England.

leone the standard monetary unit of Sierra Leone, being made up of 100 cents.

lepta a former standard monetary unit of Greece, equal to one hundredth of a DRACHMA, replaced by the Euro on January 1 2002..

lessee a person or company that is granted a LEASE.

lessor a person or company that grants a LEASE.

letter of credit a document sent from one banker to another that gives authorization for payment of a specified sum of money to the person named in the document. Letters of credit are frequently used for internationally traded goods.

letter of intent a letter in which a person formally indicates his or her serious intention to do something, such as buy a property, sign a contract, etc. Such a letter does not constitute a contract or a legal promise.

letters of administration (Brit) an order that authorizes the named person to distribute the property of a deceased person in cases where the latter has not appointed anyone else to carry out this task. The distribution of the property must be in accordance with the will of the deceased or, if he or she has died intestate, in accordance with the rules of intestacy.

leu the standard monetary unit of Moldova.

lev *see* STOTINKA.

leverage the use of borrowed money to finance expansion of a company in the hope of increasing profits.

leveraged buy-out the buy-out of one company by another by means of borrowed funds.

leveraged portfolio a high-risk PORTFOLIO that includes investments bought with borrowed money.

lex loci (Latin) the "law of the place." When making a CONTRACT, for example, it means that it is subject to the laws of the place where the contract is signed.

lex non scripta (Latin) "unwritten law."

liability a claim in respect of money borrowed on the resources of an individual or company.

liabilities in accounting, any of the debts of creditors on a business or a person.

liability insurance protection for a person or a firm against losses in the event of claims by a third party. The cover includes, for example, claims arising from negligence, such as damage or injury caused by a company's products.

libel a printed statement that defames the character or reputation of another. *See also* SLANDER.

LIBOR abbreviation, LONDON INTERBANK OFFERED RATE.

licence 1 a document giving official permission to do something, such as sell alcoholic drinks, own a firearm, drive a vehicle, etc. **2** formal permission to enter or occupy land. **3** official permission given to a manufacturer, distributor, trader, etc, to manufacture or sell a named product in a specified area for a specified time, with the LICENSEE paying either a lump sum payment and/or regular fee.

licensee a person to whom a LICENCE is granted.

lien the right of an individual to retain possession of the goods of another, who is in debt to him or her, until the debt has been settled. *See also* CARRIER'S LIEN, INNKEEPER'S LIEN, JUDGMENT LIEN, MECHANIC'S LIEN

life annuity an ANNUITY that ceases to be paid on the death of a specified person.

life insurance a form of INSURANCE by which a specified amount of money is paid on the death of the person whose life is assured. In the case of ENDOWMENT INSURANCE the money is paid either on the death of the person whose life is assured or at the end of an agreed specified period of time, whichever occurs earlier.

life insured the person who is named on a LIFE INSURANCE policy and on whose death the INSURANCE COMPANY makes a payment. The owner of the policy is not necessarily the same person as the life assured.

LIFFE the abbreviated form of **London International Financial Futures (and Options) Exchange.**

likuta (*plural* **makuta**) a monetary unit of the Democratic Republic of Congo (formerly Zaire), equivalent to one hundredth of a ZAIRE.

lilangeni the standard monetary unit of Swaziland, made up of 100 cents.

limitations of actions statutory rules that put a limit on the period of time within which a civil legal action can be brought.

limited company a company in which the liability of its members with reference to the debts of the company is limited. *See* LIMITED LIABILITY, PRIVATE LIMITED COMPANY and PUBLIC LIMITED COMPANY.

limited liability an arrangement that limits the maximum loss that a shareholder sustains in the event of the company in which he or she holds shares being wound up. The loss is limited to his or her SHARE CAPITAL and no claim can be made by CREDITORS against other ASSETS.

limited partner a partner in an enterprise who has limited legal liability for the DEBTS of the PARTNERSHIP. *See also* GENERAL PARTNER.

limited partnership a PARTNERSHIP where one or more partners have limited liability for the partnership's debts. See also GENERAL PARTNERSHIP.

line and staff management a system of management used in some large organizations in which there are two separate hierarchies of management, one made up of **line managers** and one made up of **staff managers**, although sometimes the distinction is not completely clear-cut. Line managers are involved in the achieving of the company's primary policy goals and in the running of the organization's main activities, such as production, sales, etc. Staff managers are responsible for providing advice and supporting services, such as personnel management.

line of credit an agreement between a bank and a customer that establishes the maximum amount of CREDIT that the bank will allow the customer.

line production *or* **mass production** a type of manufacturing process in which large volumes of identical, or very similar, products are made in a set sequence of operations.

line of balance chart a chart used in production scheduling that supplies data on the agreed delivery dates of products and data on the availability of the component parts that are required to manufacture the products.

lipa *see* KUNA.

liquid assets assets that are held either in the form

of cash or in the form of something that can readily be converted into cash. A company's current liquid assets in relation to their current liabilities is a guide to its level of solvency or LIQUIDITY.

liquidation the process that brings about the dissolution of a company. This often occurs because a company is insolvent, in which case the assets of the company are used to discharge as many outstanding liabilities to creditors as possible. Where the company is solvent and there is money left over after the discharge of liabilities to CREDITORS, the remaining money is divided up pro rata among the ordinary shareholders of the company. See INSOLVENCY.

liquidator a person appointed by the creditors of a company, by the shareholders or directors of a company or by a court to regulate the LIQUIDATION of the company.

liquidity the possession by a company of enough LIQUID ASSETS to discharge its debts and carry out its business.

lira 1 the former standard monetary unit of Italy and San Marino, made up of 100 CENTESIMOS, and replaced by the Euro on January 1 2002. **2** the standard monetary unit of Turkey, made up of 100 KURUS. **3** the standard monetary unit of Malta, made up of 100 cents.

lisente the standard monetary unit of Lesotho, equal to one hundredth of a LOTI.

lis pendens (Latin) "a pending lawsuit."

listed company (Brit) a company the shares of which are traded on the main market in the London Stock Exchange, subject to certain conditions being satisfied. *See* LISTING REQUIRE-MENTS.

listed stocks STOCKS that are traded on a STOCK EX-CHANGE.

listing requirements (Brit) the conditions that require to be satisfied before the SHARES of a company can be traded on the main market of the London Stock Exchange. The two main require-ments are that the value of the company's AS-SETS should exceed a certain value and that the company publish certain financial information, both at the time of the flotation and on a regu-lar basis after that.

list price 1 the retail price of a consumer article as recommended by the manufacturer and shown on the price list. Unless there is some restric-tion imposed by a price-maintenance agree-ment, the retailer may offer a discount on the list price to attract custom. **2** the price entered on an invoice by a supplier to a retailer or wholesaler before the deduction of any dis-counts.

litas the standard monetary unit of Lithuania.

litigant a party involved in a lawsuit. The litigant may be either the defendant or the plaintiff.

litigation legal action, a lawsuit.

Lloyd's (of London) a corporation that is involved in UNDERWRITING of INSURANCE. Lloyd's does not itself perform any underwriting insurance business, its member BROKERS and insurers either acting individually or acting together on a CONSORTIUM or syndicate basis. Its business comes to it from brokers who are in touch with the public, and the syndicates of underwriters are approached by the brokers and do not themselves have any contact with the public. Lloyd's underwriters have to deposit a substantial sum of money with the corporation and accept unlimited liability before they can become members. Most of the members of the syndicates are **Lloyd's names**, who are underwriting members who play no part in the business of underwriting but who share in the profits and losses of the syndicate and provide the risk capital. Lloyd's now covers all insurance risks but has long specialized in the area of marine insurance. The corporation takes its name from Edward Lloyd, the proprietor of a coffee shop in Tavern Street in the City of London, which was the origin of the corporation in 1689.

loan in finance, a transaction where one party provides money to another party on condition that it will be repaid at a certain time plus an agreed amount of INTEREST.

loan account an account that is opened by a bank for a customer who has taken out a BANK LOAN rather than taking advantage of an OVERDRAFT facility.

loan capital *or* **debt capital** money used in the financing of a company that has been borrowed from an external source for a set period of time and that is subject to payment of interest over the period of time for which the loan has been granted.

loan shark an unlicensed, and therefore unregulated, moneylender who charges extortionate rates of INTEREST.

local area network (often abbreviated to **LAN**) a network of microcomputers connected together in a localized area such as an office building. The network is used to perform routine DATA PROCESSING functions in a company.

lockbox system a method whereby the customers of a company mail payments to a dedicated postal box. The box is cleared regularly by the company's bank, which then processes the payments quickly.

lockout a form of INDUSTRIAL ACTION in which the employees are refused access to their workplace unless they agree to accept the employer's terms.

loco price a price quoted for goods that does not include loading or transport charges but is simply the price for them in the place where they are located.

logo a company or BRAND NAME that is written or illustrated in a distinctive way so that it is instantly recognized by consumers.

Lombard Street (Brit) the street in the City of London that is the center of the money market.

London Acceptance Credit (Brit) a method by which a UK exporter of goods can be supplied with immediate cash. The exporter draws a BILL OF EXCHANGE on the foreign purchaser and this bill is then pledged to a merchant bank in London which accepts an ACCOMMODATION BILL drawn by the exporter.

London Interbank Offered Rate (Brit) (commonly abbreviated to **LIBOR**) the rate of interest charged on interbank loans. It is the most important interest rate for international banks and is used as a yardstick for lending to bank customers. *See* **interbank market**.

London International Financial Futures and Options Exchange (LIFFE) (Brit) a FUTURES MARKET opened in London in 1982 and now based in the City of London. It deals in options and futures contracts, including those relating to government bonds, stock-and-share indexes, foreign currencies, etc. It was originally called the London International Financial Futures Exchange but in 1992 the London Traded Options Market merged with it and 'and Options' was added, although the abbreviation LIFFE remained the same as before.

London Stock Exchange (Brit) the market in London that deals in securities. Such dealings began in London in the seventeenth century, the name 'stock exchange' being first applied to New Jonathan's Coffee House in 1773.

long-dated gilts *or* **longs** gilt-edged securities not redeemable for fifteen years or more. *See* **gilt-edged ooourity.**

long position a situation in which the holdings of a dealer in securities, commodities, currencies, etc, exceed his or her sales, often because he or she is expecting prices to rise.

longs *see* LONG-DATED GILTS.

long-term in accounting, indicates one year or longer.

long-term liability a sum of money that is owed but does not have to be repaid within the next accounting period of a company.

loss in business, the amount by which the cost of a transaction exceeds its RETURN.

loss adjuster a person who is appointed by an insurance company to investigate and produce a report on an insurance claim made by a policy holder. The claim is settled on the basis of this report.

loss leader a product or service that is offered for

sale by a company at a loss in order to attract customers in the hope that they will buy other more profitable goods or services.

loti the standard monetary unit of Lesotho, made up of 100 LISENTE.

low balling to offer an extremely low price to a potential customer in the hope of securing a contract. This tactic is often used when a company is trying to lure the customer away from their existing supplier. Low balling is a legitimate technique, but it may rebound on the firm as they try to recoup the consequent losses by overpricing other services and applying extra charges which may not appeal to the customer.

Ltd (Brit) the usual abbreviation for LIMITED COMPANY. This must appear as part of the name of a private limited company.

lwei a monetary unit of Angola, equal to one hundredth of a KWANZA.

M

Maastricht Treaty an agreement between the member countries of the EUROPEAN UNION, signed in 1991, with the aim of providing closer unification of the economic and political systems of the member countries.

macroeconomics the study of an economic system as a whole, including money supply and its influence on prices, consumer demand, employment, savings etc.

Madison Avenue a street in New York City where many of best known advertising agencies in the United States are located.

mail float a reference to checks that are still going through the postal system.

mail order a means of selling products directly to customers through the postal service by means of catalogs.

mail shot sales or advertising material that is sent by post to a large number of people regarded as potential customers.

main market the premier market for trading in EQUITIES on the London Stock Exchange.

Main Street a term that refers to ordinary investors as compared with professional financiers and BROKERS.

maintenance of membership a clause in a union agreement that requires all workers who were members of the union at the time the agreement was made, to remain members for the lifetime of the agreement. There is usually an "escape clause" that allows workers to leave the union within a specific period of time before the agreement becomes effective.

majority shareholder a SHAREHOLDER who owns more than 50% of the voting stock of a company and therefore has a CONTROLLING INTEREST in the company.

makeready time the time necessary to install and prepare machinery for production.

makuta *see* LIKUTA, ZAIRE.

malfeasance committing an act that is wrong or that the doer has agreed not to perform. For example, as part of a CONTRACT.

malingerer a person who pretends to be ill or injured in order to avoid work.

management accounting the process of collecting and processing information relevant to accounting within an organization with a view to ensuring effective financial planning and control.

management buy-in the acquisition of a company or of a division of a company by a small group of shareholders, often ex-managers of the company, who then form part of a new management team, the buy-in often being backed by VENTURE CAPITAL.

management buy-out the acquisition of a company or a division of a company by members of its existing management team.

management by exception a management system by which only important variations from plan or budget are brought to the attention of senior management, routine decisions being made further down the line.

management by walking around a management system that involves managers spending time walking around the factory or office, thereby having the opportunity to communicate regularly with the staff on an informal basis.

management consultant a professional adviser who specializes in giving advice to organizations on ways of improving their business efficiency and profitability, for example by giving recommendations on business strategy and organizational structure.

managing director the director in a company who has the responsibility for the day-to-day running of the company. *See also* CHIEF EXECUTIVE.

manat the standard monetary unit of Azerbaijan and Turkmenistan, made up of 100 gopik.

mandamus (Latin) "we command." A court order of the highest authority that requires a person or an organization to perform a certain act.

manifest a detailed, official list of goods carried as cargo on a ship or airplane.

manpower 1 the available labor force in a particular area (refers to both men and women). **2** a reference to all workers at whatever level in an organization (refers to both men and women).

manufacturer's suggested retail price (MSRP) the prices at which a manufacturer suggests that its products are sold. The retailer is not, however, compelled to sell at these prices.

margin the difference between the selling price and the cost price of goods or services.

marginal revenue the extra revenue that is obtained by a firm from the sale of an additional unit of production.

market cannibalization the impact a company's new product may have on the sales of its existing products. For example, the introduction of a new candy bar may reduce the sales of a company's existing range of candy bars.

market challenger a firm that is ranked second in terms of the market share of a product and that may be in a position to challenge the position of the MARKET LEADER by the mounting of an aggressive campaign.

market development a sales strategy undertaken by a firm that aims at extending the sales of existing products in new markets.

market forces the forces of supply and demand that in a free market determine such things as the price at which a product is offered and the quantity of a product that is available.

marketing the process relating to the various steps involved in identifying and satisfying customers' needs, including MARKETING RESEARCH, new PRODUCT DEVELOPMENT, pricing, promotion, DISTRIBUTION and selling.

marketing audit a review of a firm's MARKETING capabilities by assessing its strengths and weaknesses.

marketing mix the factors that are important to a firm in marketing its products to consumers. These include the product, the price, the promotion and the place where the product is sold.

marketing research the systematic collection, classification and analysis of information relating to MARKETING considerations and problems in order to reduce the possibility of inappropriate or unprofitable marketing activity.

marketing strategy a strategy employed by a firm in order to identify and achieve its MARKETING objectives.

market leader the seller of a product that has the largest share of a market.

market-maker (Brit) a dealer on the London Stock Exchange who buys and sells securities as a principal and is obliged to announce prices at which he will undertake to buy or sell a particular SECURITY at a particular time.

market segment a part of a market that differs from other parts in terms of customer profile, buying pattern, etc, and therefore can be targeted by separate marketing campaigns, etc.

market segmentation the division of a market into MARKET SEGMENTS.

market share the proportion of total sales of a product in a market that is achieved by one brand or company.

market-skimming pricing a pricing policy that involves the setting of a relatively high price for a product in order to make high PROFIT MARGINS.

market value the amount for which a firm's ASSETS could be sold on the open market.

marking-up (Brit) the raising of prices by MARKET-MAKERS on the London Stock Exchange in expectation of an increased demand for a particular SECURITY.

markka the former standard monetary unit of Finland, made up of 100 PENNIA, and replaced by the Euro on January 1 2002..

mark-up the amount by which the cost of goods or services is increased when the selling price is established.

mass production *see* LINE PRODUCTION.

materials cost the money that is spent by a firm

on its direct materials or indirect materials, the amount spent on direct materials being considered to be part of PRIME COST and the amount spent on indirect materials being considered to be a manufacturing OVERHEAD.

materials handling in manufacturing, the process of moving materials, such as packing, transporting and storing.

materials management the administration and control of the materials used by a firm in a production process.

mature in finance, to expire, to cease to exist.

matrix organization an organization structure in a firm in which some employees report to managers in more than one department.

maturity date the date on which a BOND, BILL OF EXCHANGE, INSURANCE POLICY, etc, becomes due for payment.

measured day work a system of calculating wages in which a daily wage is agreed on the basis of a set daily production target.

mechanic's lien a legally enforceable claim against a property that can be made by someone who has worked on it or provided materials for its improvement, in the event of non-payment for the work done or materials supplied. *See also* CARRIER'S LIEN, INNKEEPER'S LIEN, JUDGMENT LIEN, LIEN.

mediation the intervention in an INDUSTRIAL

DISPUTE of a neutral third party who acts as a go-between to the parties in the dispute with the object of getting the parties to reach a compromise solution.

member bank a bank that belongs to a clearing system or central banking system.

member firm a firm of BROKERS or MARKET-MAKERS that is a member of the London Stock Exchange.

memorandum of association (Brit) an official document that is completed by a company and filed with the REGISTRAR OF COMPANIES. The memorandum is signed by the subscribers who formed the company and contains the company's name, a statement that the company is a public company, a statement of LIMITED LIABILITY, the address of the registered office of the company, the objects of the company, the amount of authorized share capital and the division of this and the amount of the guarantee.

merchandizing the in-store promotion by a retailer of selected products, consisting, for example, of POINT-OF-SALE DISPLAY materials and special buying incentives, such as free samples and gifts and temporary price reductions.

merchant bank a bank that originally specialized in the provision of finance for merchants, often being involved in foreign trade. The merchant bank then functioned as an

ACCEPTANCE HOUSE. In recent times, however, the merchant banks have diversified and now offer a whole range of financial services to clients. Such services include the provision of VENTURE CAPITAL, investment management, stockbroking and the provision of advice on MERGERS and TAKEOVER BIDS.

merger the combination of two or more firms into a single business on a basis that is given mutual agreement by the management of the relevant firms and is given the approval of the relevant shareholders.

method study the analysis and recording of ways of carrying out tasks with a view to maximizing the efficiency of these methods.

metical *see* CENTAVO.

middleman a person or firm that acts as an intermediary between the producer or seller of goods or services and the buyer of these goods and services, the middleman making a profit in the process.

middle management a member of the management team who occupies a middle position in the management hierarchy of a firm, those involved in middle management being below the level of senior managers who are concerned with business strategy.

middle management obsolescence a reference to the way in which the widespread use of the computer has eroded the authority and usefulness of MIDDLE MANAGEMENT by changing the way decisions are made.

middle price the price of a SECURITY, COMMODITY or currency that lies halfway between the offer price or selling price and the BID PRICE or buying price.

milime *see* DINAR 3.

minimum lending rate *see* BANK RATE.

mission statement a formal statement of the aims of a firm.

mixed economy a country's economy in which some goods and services are produced by means of state-owned organizations and some by private enterprise firms.

modeling a method of representing an actual, or possible future, state of affairs. For example, a model of the previous year's financial statement might be used to aid future planning. Models can be depicted as graphs, pictures or as mathematical representations of a situation.

monetary control the employment of a central bank of a country by the government of that country to control the money supply.

monetary gold gold held by the government as an ASSET.

monetary policy governmental control of the country's currency especially through the supply of money.

monetary system 1 the system that is used by a country to implement its monetary policy, to provide money for internal use and to control the exchange of its own currency with the currencies of foreign countries. **2** a system used to control the exchange rate of a group of countries, as in the EUROPEAN MONETARY SYSTEM.

monetary unit the standard unit of currency in a particular country.

money center banks banks that are located in major financial centers and raise most of their funds from MONEY MARKETS rather than from depositors.

money market a market that is engaged in the short-term lending and borrowing of money and that links the various financial institutions, such as banks, discount houses, acceptance houses, companies and the government.

money market funds MUTUAL FUNDS that place their money in short-term, generally safe, investments such as US government SECURITIES.

money supply the stock of money that is in a country's economy, often the quantity of money issued by a country's central bank.

mongo a Mongolian monetary unit equal to one hundredth of a TUGRIK.

Monopolies and Mergers Commission (Brit) a regulatory body in the UK the remit of which is to investigate and report on cases of MONOPOLY,

MERGERS, TAKEOVER BIDS and anti-competitive practices referred to it by the OFFICE OF FAIR TRADING, with a view to determining whether any of the referred cases involves operations that are against the public interest.

monopolistic competition a situation where there are only a limited number of producers of a particular product or service. In such a situation consumers will have less influence on price than producers.

monopoly a market structure in which there is only one supplier or producer.

monopsony a market in which there is only a single buyer.

moonlighting having more than one job.

moral hazard the possibility that dishonest or careless behavior by an insured party will increase the risk of a claim. For example, a company insured against loss from fire may take fewer fire precautions than if it had no fire insurance.

mortgage the advance of a LOAN to a person or firm, called the mortgagor or borrower, by another person or organization, usually a financial institution such as a bank or SAVINGS AND LOAN ASSOCIATION, called the mortgagee or lender, the loan being used to acquire an ASSET, usually a piece of property such as a house, office or factory. The mortgage is repaid over a fixed period, such as 25 years. Borrowers may elect to have a repayment mortgage under which capital and interest are paid to the mortgagee or they may elect to pay only the interest to the mortgagee, with other arrangements, such as an endowment policy, being made to repay the capital.

mortgagee a person or company that lends money against the security of a property.

mortgage rate the interest rate on a MORTGAGE loan.

mortgagor the borrower of money secured against a property.

multilateral netting a financial arrangement under which two or more associated companies may offset their receipts and payments with each other and thus arrive at a single net intercompany payment or receipt balance.

multinational enterprise a corporation that has production centers in more than one country.

multiple exchange rate an exchange rate that has more than one value, depending on what the relevant currency is to be used for. For example, a country with a multiple exchange rate might have a specially favorable rate for tourists and a less favorable rate for commercial purposes.

multiple listing where REAL ESTATE BROKERS agree to provide information about REAL ESTATE listings to each other. Each firm in the agreement lists the same properties and has an equal chance to sell them. The original listing broker and the selling broker usually share the commission on a sale.

multiple-unit pricing a pricing system under which more than one unit of a product is sold at a price that is lower than the total price of the individual units. Thus a supermarket that is offering customers a deal under which they buy two of a product and get one free is thereby operating a system of multiple-unit pricing.

municipal bond a BOND issued by state or local authorities and on which the INTEREST earned is usually tax free.

Murphy's Law the theory, put forward by Ed Murphy, an engineer, in 1949, that if anything can go wrong it will go wrong.

mutual fund where an investment company pools money from several investors and invests the money in specific types of SECURITIES. A mutual fund company provides investment services for small investors. MONEY MARKET FUNDS are a form of mutual fund.

mystery shopper a person who is hired to act as a customer in a store or other facility and who evaluates staff performance, pricing, cleanliness etc. Mystery shoppers never identify themselves and staff never know who they are.

N

NAFTA the common abbreviated form of NORTH AMERICAN FREE TRADE AREA.

naira the monetary unit of Nigeria, made up of 100 KOBO.

naive quantitative methods methods that are used to obtain a forecast of future trends of some kind, such as the likely demand for a product, which use historical data in, for example, the calculation of an average of past demand.

NASDAQ (National Association of Securities Dealers Automatic Quotation System) a system that provides price quotes for the OVER-THE-COUNTER market.

national bank a US commercial bank established by means of a Federal charter, which requires it to be a member of the FEDERAL RESERVE SYSTEM.

national debt the money that is owed by a government to domestic and overseas lenders.

National Consumer Council (Brit) an organization, set up by the UK government in 1975 and funded by the Department of Trade and Industry, that is intended to protect consumer interests and represent the consumer in matters of policy.

national income the total monetary value of the income brought in by a country's economic activity over one year.

national income accounts a financial statement of the total income that is generated in a country's economy over a set period of time, usually one year.

national insurance contributions (Brit) payments that are made by employers and employees to the UK government to finance benefits, such as unemployment benefit, sick pay, invalidity benefit and retirement pensions. There are four classes of contribution, Class 1 being subdivided, and they are categorized by the type of earned income received by the relevant person.

nationalization the process of bringing the ASSETS of a company under the control of the state instead of private ownership. The companies involved are usually those considered to be strategically important to the country and are often acquired by the state through COMPULSORY PURCHASE. The process of nationalization is often related to political ideology.

National Labor Relations Board (NLRB) first established in 1935, the NLRB oversees relations between employers and representatives of employees, and resolves disputes involving unfair labor practices and so on.

National Savings Certificates (Brit) certificates issued by the government as part of a savings incentive scheme for personal savers which also raises money for the government. The certificates are issued by post offices and banks and the interest gained on the savings is free of income tax.

national savings market includes all savings made by individuals and organizations such as commercial banks, deposits in savings banks, shares in savings and loan associations, life insurance reserves and so on.

National Savings Stock Register (Brit) a government-run organization that allows members of the public to purchase certain Treasury stock and some other GILT-EDGED SECURITIES by post directly without having to use the services of a stockbroker.

natural wastage the process by which a firm or organization can decrease in size without the necessity of resorting to redundancy. Natural wastage covers members of staff who have reached retirement age, those who have died or been declared unfit for work and those who, for some reason or other, have decided to resign.

NDP the abbreviated form of NET DOMESTIC PRODUCT.

near money an ASSET that can be used almost as if it was money, although it is not. For example, a government BOND can be converted into cash very quickly.

needs analysis a method of deciding what training is necessary for new and existing employees.

negative cash flow a CASH FLOW in which the outgoings exceed the income.

negative income tax a form of taxation aimed at improving the lot of the less well off. It involves establishing an acceptable threshold level of income for everyone and then taxing those who earn above that amount at a progressive rate in the usual manner of income tax and compensating those who earn less than that amount by giving them tax credits or rebates.

negative leadership the control and motivation of people by means of punishment or the threat of punishment.

negotiable in finance, transferable, cashable or exchangeable.

negotiation a process by which two or more parties attempt to reach agreement and resolve a conflict of interest, such as the amount of a pay agreement.

nepotism preferential treatment of family members or friends, especially in employment.

net the term used to refer to an amount that remains after certain deductions have been made.

net assets the assets of a company, including FIXED ASSETS and NET CURRENT ASSETS, or WORKING CAPITAL, less current liabilities.

net asset value the value of a SHARE in a company, which is obtained by dividing the amount assigned to the NET ASSETS of the company by the number of shares that have been issued.

net book value the value at which an ASSET appears in the financial records of a firm, usually as at the date of the last balance sheet. This repre sents its original value or cost less any depreciation that has occurred since its purchase or last revaluation.

net current assets the current ASSETS of a company less its current LIABILITIES. Since the amount resulting from this exercise is the amount of capital that is constantly in use in the course of the company's trading, it is known as WORKING CAPITAL or circulating capital.

net dividend the DIVIDEND that a company pays to its SHAREHOLDERS after the exclusion of the tax credit received by the shareholders.

net domestic product (often abbreviated to **NDP**) the GROSS DOMESTIC PRODUCT after the deduction of CAPITAL CONSUMPTION, i.e. depreciation during the relevant period.

net income 1 a person's income after INCOME TAX has been deducted. **2** the income of a person or organization that remains after the deduction of the expenses that have had to be met in earning it.

net interest the interest that is paid into a bank or building society savings account after tax has been deducted at source.

net lease a leasing agreement that makes the lessee responsible for all relevant taxes, maintenance, insurance and any other costs associated with the ASSET.

net national product (often abbreviated to **NNP**) the amount that remains after the CAPITAL CONSUMPTION, i.e. the total depreciation in the value of capital goods, has been deducted from the GROSS NATIONAL PRODUCT, being equal to the amount of money that is available in a country's economy for expenditure on goods and services.

net present value (often abbreviated to **NPV**) in discounted CASH FLOWS, the difference between the present value of the cash outflow and that of the cash inflow.

net price the price that a purchaser pays for goods after the deduction of any discounts.

net profit 1 the profit that a company makes after all running costs and expenses have been taken into account. **2** the final profit that a company makes after all relevant taxes have been deducted from net profit 1.

net realizable value (often abbreviated to **NRV**) the amount for which the stock of a company can be sold, less the costs likely to be involved in carrying out the sale.

net receipts the total amount of money received by a company or in a business transaction after the deduction of costs, raw materials, relevant taxation, etc.

net return the profit that is made on any form of investment after the deduction of all expenses.

network analysis/modeling a method of planning, scheduling and controlling complex projects that involves various interrelated but distinct elements of work known as activities.

networking 1 a method of organizing work in which some tasks are undertaken by people who work away from the office or main place of work, often at home and frequently on a self-employed basis, but who are connected to the main company center by computer-based information links, such as E-MAIL. **2** the process of linking together a series of personal computers. **3** the linking of a number of firms or of a number of units in a firm involved in the complete manufacturing and marketing processes of a product. **4** the establishment of contacts with other people whose business expertise, knowledge, experience and contacts might prove useful.

net worth the value of a company when its LIABILITIES have been deducted from its ASSETS, especially when these are assessed at their true market value. *See also* OWNER'S EQUITY.

new issue a SHARE that is being offered for sale on a STOCK EXCHANGE for the first time.

new sol the standard monetary unit of Peru, which is made up of 100 cents.

ngultrum *see* CHETRUM.

ngwee a monetary unit of Zambia that is worth one hundredth of a KWACHA.

niche marketing a form of MARKETING that involves a comparatively small segment of a market, sometimes a specialist one, with its own distinctive customer profile and buyer characteristics.

Nikkei Index a Japanese share index by which changes in the aggregate value of a particular 'basket' of company shares are measured. It is the Japanese equivalent of the UK FINANCIAL TIMES SHARE INDEX and the US DOW-JONES INDUSTRIAL AVERAGE. Nikkei is a shortened form of the financial newspaper group, Nikon Keizai Shimbun.

nil basis the basis on which the earnings per share of a company is worked out, taking into account only the constant elements in the tax charge of the relevant company.

ninety-day letter a communication from the INTERNAL REVENUE SERVICE advising of nonpayment of taxes. The taxpayer must pay the taxes within 90 days or take the matter to court.

NNP the abbreviated form of NET NATIONAL PRODUCT.

no-claim bonus a discount given on PREMIUMS, particularly car-insurance premiums, to policyholders by insurance companies as a reward for not claiming on their insurance.

nolo contendere (Latin) "I do not want to contend." This means that a defendant in a criminal case does not wish to contest the charges, but it does not carry an admission of guilt.

nominal accounts ledger accounts that do not bear the name of an individual or organization but relate to concepts. These include items of income, such as rents from properties received by a company or expenses incurred in the running of a company, such as rates, lighting, heating, etc.

nominal ledger the ledger that is used to record NOMINAL ACCOUNTS as distinct from personal ledgers, which contain the accounts of individual customers and suppliers respectively.

nominal yield *see* COUPON RATE.

nonconforming goods products that do not meet the standards stipulated in a CONTRACT and will therefore be rejected by the customer.

noncontributory retirement plan a PENSION PLAN to which the employer makes all the contributions.

nonexecutive director a member of the board of

directors of a company who is not employed by the company and who is not involved in its day-to-day running, but who supplies independent judgment or specialist expertise in return for a director's fee.

nonprofit corporation a corporation that is not permitted to make a PROFIT and does not have stockholders.

non-recourse finance a bank LOAN in which the bank issuing the loan is entitled to repayment only from the PROFITS of the scheme that the loan is being used to finance and not from any other resources of the borrower.

non-statutory accounts a BALANCE SHEET or PROFIT AND LOSS ACCOUNT that relates to a financial period of a company that does not form part of the STATUTORY ACCOUNTS.

nonvoting stock the holders of such SHARES do not have any voting rights at the company's ANNUAL GENERAL MEETING.

no-par a term used to describe a SECURITY that has no PAR VALUE.

no-par value stock SHARES that have 'no-par value' printed on the SHARE CERTIFICATE.

North American Free Trade Agreement (NAFTA) a FREE TRADE agreement signed in 1989 by the USA and Canada and extended to include Mexico in 1994.

no-strike agreement an agreement drawn up by an

employer and LABOR UNION by which the labor union undertakes not to instigate or support a STRIKE by the employees of the company.

nostro account (Brit) a bank account that is conducted by a UK bank in another country, usually in the currency of that country.

notional income income that is not actually received, although it is a possibility that it might be deemed to be so for INCOME TAX purposes. An example of notional income might be the interest that has been dispensed with on an interest-free loan.

novation the replacement of one legal agreement by another, subject to the agreement of the parties involved.

NPV the abbreviated form of NET PRESENT VALUE.

NRV the abbreviated form of NET REALIZABLE VALUE.

numbered account a bank account that is identified only by a number rather than by a name and number. Numbered accounts are usually located outside the US and are often used to conceal money.

numeraire a monetary unit that is used to value international transactions in goods and services and intergovernmental financial settlements on a common basis.

O

objective and task method a method of managing and budgeting that involves the formulation of specific objectives and the setting out of and costing of the tasks, which have to be completed in order to meet these objectives.

objectivity in accounting terms a principle that seeks to minimize any subjectivity or personal judgment affecting the recording and summarizing of financial transactions on the part of the person undertaking the preparation of the records.

obligation the duty to fulfill an agreement, for example to pay a DEBT.

obsolescence a reduction in the value of a FIXED ASSET because of its age. It may still be functioning well but may have become out of date because of improvements in technology or because of changes of fashion in CONSUMER DURABLES.

Occupational Safety and Health Administration (OSHA) a sector of the US Department of Labor that sets and enforces health and safety standards in the workplace.

occupational pension a pension scheme that is operated by employers and to which employers and employees both make regular contributions to a pension fund or insurance company scheme, the employee on retirement receiving a pension in relation to the amount of his or her contributions.

odd lot a transaction for fewer than 100 shares. *See also* ROUND LOT.

OECD the abbreviated form of ORGANIZATION FOR ECONOMIC COOPERATION AND DEVELOPMENT.

off-balance sheet financing a method of financing a company's business activities so that some of the finance and assets do not appear on the balance sheet. The payment for the use of a piece of equipment, such as a computer, by hiring or leasing it rather than buying it outright can be regarded as an example. The hire cost will appear as an annual operating cost and set against profits but the computer will not appear as a FIXED ASSET since the company do not own the computer.

offer by prospectus an offer of a new issue of shares by a company made directly to the public by means of a prospectus which sets out details of the company, such as its past trading record and its CAPITAL STRUCTURE.

offer for sale a method of raising new SHARE CAPITAL by offering and issuing new SHARES to members of the general public. These are often offered through an intermediary such as a merchant bank or ISSUING HOUSE.

official reserves holdings of gold and foreign currencies by official institutions.

off the books a transaction that is not recorded. Such transactions are often made to avoid paying tax.

observed time the time taken by an operator to perform a task when under observation as part of a TIME AND MOTION STUDY.

Office of Fair Trading (Brit) a government department, established in 1973 and headed by the Director General of Fair Trading, which aims to protect the consumer against unfair trading practices, such as the false description of goods and inaccurate weights and measures. It also administers in the UK the competition policy as set out by the EUROPEAN COMMISSION, being responsible for MONOPOLIES and MERGERS, RESTRICTIVE TRADE PRACTICES, consumer affairs, consumer credit and anti-competitive practices.

Official List (Brit) 1 a list of all the securities traded on the main market of the London Stock Exchange. **2** a list prepared daily by the London Stock Exchange which records all the sales in listed securities which have taken place during the day and gives prices and dividend dates.

official receiver (Brit) an officer of the court who is appointed by the government to act as a receiver in bankruptcy and winding-up cases. *See* RECEIVERSHIP.

off-line referring to computing equipment which is not connected to the central processing computing unit.

off-line reader a computer program which allows users to be connected to an ON-LINE computing system and to download any e-mail messages to their own machine.

offset 1 a code on the magnetic strip of a plastic card which, in conjunction with a **personal identification number (PIN)**, acts as verification that the person who is using it has the right to do so. **2** the right of a bank to seize any bank account balances of a debtor or guarantor who has failed to meet LOAN obligations.

offshore banking banking services in places which offer non-residents tax advantages in a legal way. They are informally known as TAX HAVENS

offshore fund a fund held by a financial institution that has its registered office in a TAX HAVEN. *See* OFFSHORE BANKING.

Old Lady of Threadneedle Street a reference to the Bank of England in London, one of the oldest CENTRAL BANKS in the world.

oligopoly a kind of market structure in which relatively few sellers supply the needs of a large number of buyers.

ombudsman an official in charge of a body which is responsible for settling disputes between suppliers of services or goods and those who use them. The idea originated in Sweden, and referred to a government official who was charged with investigating complaints from the public.

omnibus research a method of MARKETING RESEARCH based on questionnaires with several parts which are sent out on a regular basis to a panel of people who fill them in. Space on the questionnaires can be allotted to companies which have a limited number of questions on which they are seeking advice or to those which have very specific marketing questions, thus allowing them the benefit of marketing research without the cost and effort of setting up a separate questionnaire.

on-line referring to computer equipment which is connected to a central processing unit.

on stream where an investment appears to be performing in line with the investor's expectations.

OPEC the abbreviated form of ORGANIZATION OF PETROLEUM EXPORTING COUNTRIES.

open-end fund a MUTUAL FUND with an unlimited number of SHARES.

opening price the price at which the first bids and offers were made or at which the first transactions were agreed.

open-market operations the buying or selling of government bonds and treasury bills as a means of controlling the money supply.

open-market value the value of an ASSET, which is equal to the amount of money that a willing purchaser would be prepared to pay a willing seller at a particular time.

open-pricing agreement an agreement among firms operating in an OLIGOPOLY by which a list of prices and intended price changes is circulated to those firms involved with a view to avoiding a PRICE WAR.

operating budget a forecast of the financial needs of a company or organization required for its future trading over a fixed period, usually a year. It involves working out likely sales, production, cash flow, etc, and alterations can be made to it in the course of the period of time if the forecast of these does not prove to be accurate.

operating lease a form of LEASE under which a FIXED ASSET is hired out to an individual or firm for a period of time that is considerably shorter than the likely length of its useful economic life.

operational research a method of tackling industrial and commercial problems or issues using scientific and mathematical techniques, the aim being to establish an optimal level of efficiency.

opportunity cost the financial advantage that is foregone if a firm opts for one form of action or activity rather than another using the same resources. For example, the operating cost of manufacturing a line of one particular item of furniture might be measured against the profits that might be made if a line of a different item of furniture was manufactured by the same factory using exactly the same resources.

optimized production technology a computer-based system for planning production and the assigning of resources.

option the right to purchase or sell a fixed amount of a COMMODITY, SECURITY or currency at a particular price on a particular date. An option to purchase is known as a **call option** and an option to sell is known as a **put option**.

optional extra a feature that can be added to a product to enhance its appearance or performance but is not part of the basic or standard model.

option to purchase 1 a right that is given to shareholders to buy shares in certain companies under certain circumstances at a reduced price. **2** a right that is purchased by or given to a person at a specified price on or before an arranged date with the undertaking that the seller will not sell it to anyone else or withdraw it from sale before that date.

oral contract an agreement that is not written down. Oral contracts are usually legally valid but difficult to enforce.

order of business the order of the items to be dealt with on the agenda of a business meeting.

ordinary share a unit of the SHARE CAPITAL of a company. Ordinary shares are issued to individuals or institutions, which provide long-term capital to a company. They yield DIVIDENDS based on the NET PROFIT of the company. Shares in publicly owned quoted companies are usually traded on STOCK EXCHANGES.

ordinary shareholders those who hold ORDINARY SHARES. They are paid DIVIDENDS on the SHARES that they hold and, in the event of the company being wound up, they are entitled to any remaining ASSETS of the business after all debts and the claims of PREFERENCE SHAREHOLDERS have been met. Ordinary shareholders usually have voting rights at the company's ANNUAL GENERAL MEETING.

ore *see* KRONA, KRONE.

organic growth the genuine growth rate of an organization, without taking into account such events as MERGERS, takeovers and so on.

organization chart a chart or diagram that illustrates the structure and chain of responsibility of a company.

Organization for Economic Cooperation and Development (OECD)

Organization of the Petroleum Exporting Countries (often abbreviated to **OPEC**) an organization that

217

was founded in 1960 to coordinate the petroleum policies of the member countries and to protect their individual and collective interests.

original goods natural products that have no commercial value until they have been subjected to some kind of production process.

ouguiya the standard monetary unit of Mauritania, being made up of 5 KHOUMS.

outplacement counseling services provided to people who are terminated.

output tax the tax that is added by a trader to the price of the goods or services that he or she supplies.

outside broker a stockbroker who is not a member of the STOCK EXCHANGE but is an intermediary between a member of the public and a broker who is a member of the stock exchange.

outsourcing the buying-in by a company of components, finished products, services, etc, from an external source rather than supplying these internally.

outstanding shares SHARES currently owned by investors.

outwork work that is carried out on the worker's own premises rather than those of the company for whom he or she is working.

overage too much of something. For example, an overage in a particular product would mean an overproduction of that product.

overcapacity a situation in which a firm or industry has more capacity for production than is called for by market demand.

overdraft a form of credit facility that allows the holder of a bank CHECKING ACCOUNT to let the account go into debit up to an agreed limit, interest being charged on the daily debit balance.

overhead *or* **overhead cost** a cost that is not directly related to the materials or labor directly concerned with a product. Overheads include such costs as factory heating, lighting and power, distribution costs, administration costs and research and development costs.

overhead-cost variance the difference between the actual overhead cost of a product and that which was budgeted for by the company.

overperform where a SECURITY is expected to rise in value at a faster rate than that currently prevailing in the STOCK MARKET as a whole.

override extra money paid to salespeople over and above their regular commission or salary.

Overseas Development Administration (Brit) the UK government department that deals with the administration of financial and technical aid to overseas countries.

oversold 1 where a manufacturer cannot fulfill orders by the due date for whatever reason. **2**

in the STOCK MARKET, where prices have fallen faster than value.

oversubscription a situation that occurs when a new share issue results in there being more applications for the shares than there are shares available.

over-the-counter market (OTC) a decentralized investment market over a wide geographical area where dealers are linked electronically. The OTC market sells SECURITIES not listed on the NEW YORK STOCK EXCHANGE.

overtrading a trading situation in which a company expands its production and sales beyond the resources of its WORKING CAPITAL and which can lead to liquidity problems.

overvalued where the price of an investment does not reflect its true value.

own-brand product a product that is sold under a retailer's or distributor's own name or TRADEMARK. Such products are made specially for the retailer but the manufacturers who produce them often also manufacture their own branded goods which compete in the marketplace with the retailer's own brand products. The own-brand products are usually sold cheaper than other products.

owner's equity the total ASSETS of a business organization, less its total LIABILITIES. See also NET WORTH.

own shares purchase the buying by a company of its own shares. Such a purchase is quite legal, subject to certain conditions laid out in the Companies Act.

P

pa'anga the standard monetary unit of Tonga, made up of 100 SENITI.

Pac-Man strategy in a hostile takeover situation, when the organization that is the subject of a hostile bid (the TARGET COMPANY), retaliates against the firm making the bid, launching its own TAKEOVER BID against that firm.

paid-in capital CAPITAL acquired from stockholders. Paid-in capital should be distinguished from capital generated by earnings.

paisa 1 a monetary unit of India, Nepal and Pakistan, equal to one-hundredth of a RUPEE. **2** a monetary unit of Bangladesh, equal to one hundredth of a TAKA.

paper profit a profit that is indicated by the financial records of a company but that may not in fact be a realizable profit. This can occur for various reasons, such as the value of an asset falling below its book value, because an asset that indicates a nominal profit in the company records has not actually been sold and might not achieve the price estimated if it was sold, etc.

paper loss a loss that is indicated by the financial records of a company but is not realized, i.e. it has not been paid out in cash.

para a monetary unit of Bosnia-Herzegovina and Serbia, equal to one hundredth of a DINAR.

par bond a FINANCIAL SECURITY that is bought and sold at face value and not at a discount or premium.

parenting the manner in which senior management of a company manage their subsidiary companies.

parent company a company that owns or controls one or more separate companies.

parking violation in a hostile TAKEOVER BID situation, the company which intends making an unwelcome offer gathers significant amounts of stock in the TARGET COMPANY, but arranges for it to be held by an unrelated third party. Thus the acquiring company prepares for a takeover without the target company being aware of it. Concealing ownership in this way is, however, illegal.

Parkinson's Law a theory that work expands so as to fill the time available for its completion. The theory was put forward by C. Northcote Parkinson, a British writer.

partnership a business association of two or more people formed to own and control a company. Generally, partners are responsible for the debts of the firm.

par value the nominal price of a share or other financial security, the actual market value of the share being subject to MARKET FORCES.

pass a dividend to decide not to pay a DIVIDEND.

past due a financial obligation that has not been paid by the agreed payment date.

pataca the standard monetary unit of Macao, made up of 100 AVOS.

patent a grant of exclusive ownership rights granted by the government through the US Patent Office in respect of a new invention. It gives inventors the exclusive right to make and sell their inventions. A patent lasts for 17 years.

patent pending a statement from the US Patent Office that a search is being undertaken to make sure that the PATENT is new. This must be established without doubt before the invention is officially patented.

pattern bargaining in labor relations, when a union negotiates a contract with the main company in an industry, and this contract then sets the pattern for all other companies in that sector.

payable to be paid in the future.

payback period the period of time that is required for a project to repay its original capital outlay.

pay differential the difference between the rates of pay of different groups of workers.

payee the person or entity who is to be paid.

payer the person or entity who pays.

payload that portion of a cargo that produces revenue.

payment by results a system of paying workers in which wages are directly related to performance or output.

payment date the date on which each registered SHAREHOLDER of a company will be mailed a check for the declared DIVIDEND.

payment float checks written on a company account that have not yet cleared.

peak the transitional stage from the end of a period of economic expansion to the beginning of an economic contraction.

pegging 1 the fixing of the value of a country's currency on foreign exchange markets. **2** the fixing by government order of wages or prices at their existing level in order to prevent them rising excessively during a period of INFLATION.

penni a monetary unit of Finland, equal to one hundredth of a MARKKA.

penny 1 a monetary unit of the UK, equal to one hundredth of a POUND. **2** a former monetary unit of the Republic of Ireland, equal to one hundredth of a PUNT, replaced by the Euro on January 1 2002..

penny stock high-risk, low-priced STOCK. Penny stock offers opportunities for people who do not have much money but would like to invest in the STOCK MARKET. Penny stock range in price from a few cents to a few dollars.

pension a payment received by people who have retired from employment or who have reached a certain age. Pensions are usually paid on a regular basis, either weekly or monthly, although they can take the form of a lump sum.

Pension Benefit Guaranty Corporation (PBGC) a Federal agency that insures the benefits of PENSION PLAN contributors.

pension fund money from state and private pension contributions that is invested so as to obtain as high a return as possible to provide the funds from which pensions are paid.

pension plan funds secured for the payment of retirement benefits.

per capita income the per capita income of a country indicates the average income per person. The figure is calculated by dividing the national income of a country by its total population.

percentage of sales method a rule-of-thumb method of establishing a company's promotion budget in which the budgeted amount is a set percentage of the past sales or projected sales of the relevant product.

performance appraisal the process of evaluating the performance of an employee by management with a view to deciding such things as level of pay, career prospects, potential training, etc.

period bill a BILL OF EXCHANGE that is payable on a specified date rather than on demand.

period of grace the time that is usually allowed for certain BILLS OF EXCHANGE after they mature.

perks see PERQUISITES.

permanent interest-bearing share a fixed-interest SECURITY that is non-redeemable and that pays INTEREST at a fixed rate at issue.

permission to deal permission granted by the London Stock Exchange to deal in the shares of a newly floated company.

perpetual inventory a system of continuous STOCK CONTROL in which an account is kept of each item of stock, one side of the account registering the deliveries of stock and the other side registering the issues from stock. The balance provides at any given time the number of items in stock and their value.

perquisites (perks) benefits, such as the use of a company car or expense account for personal use, offered to certain employees in addition to standard salaries and benefits.

personal account an account in a company's ledger that carries the name of an individual or organization and records the state of indebtedness of the person or organization to the company or the state of indebtedness of the company to the individual or organization, whichever is relevant.

personnel management *same as* HUMAN RESOURCE MANAGEMENT.

peseta the former standard monetary unit of Spain and Andorra, made up of 100 CENTIMOS, replaced by the Euro on January 1 2002.

pesewa a monetary unit of Ghana, equal to one hundredth of a cedi.

peso 1 the standard monetary unit of Argentina, Chile, Colombia, Cuba, the Dominican Republic, Guinea-Buissau, Mexico and the Philippines, made up of 100 CENTAVOS. **2** the standard monetary unit of Uruguay, made up of 100 CENTESIMOS.

Peter Principle a theory that maintains that, in a hierarchical organization, people rise to their own level of incompetence. The Peter Principle was put forward by Lawrence J. Peter.

petty cash the amount of cash that is held on the premises by an organization to pay for small items of expenditure.

Pfennig a former monetary unit of Germany, equal to one hundredth of a DEUTSCHMARK, replaced by the Euro on January 1 2002.

Phillips curve a graph that represents the theory, put forward by the economist A.W.H. Phillips, that as the unemployment rate decreases, the inflation rate rises at a faster rate.

phony dividend a DIVIDEND payment made from the

funds received from the sale of a NEW ISSUE of STOCK. Phony dividends are illegal.

physical capital items that are used in the production of goods and services, as opposed to financial capital. Examples of physical capital include plant, machinery and buildings.

piastre a monetary unit of Egypt, Lebanon, the Sudan and Syria, equal to one hundredth of a POUND.

picketing a form of INDUSTRIAL ACTION in which employees during a STRIKE form a **picket line** outside a factory or other place of work in order to try to prevent people entering the work premises, or to discourage customers from patronizing a firm. In the US, picketing is legal as long as picketers respect certain guidelines.

piecework work that is paid for according to a system by which pay is directly related to work done and not related to the time taken to carry out the work.

pie chart a chart that portrays visually a representation of the proportions into which something is divided. The chart consists of a circle, supposedly representing a pie, with the circle being divided into sectors or 'slices', each representing a proportion of the whole.

piggyback in railroad transportation, where truck trailers are transported on railroad cars as near as possible to their final destination, then unloaded and delivered by local trucking companies.

piracy an example of illegal infringement of COPYRIGHT.

pit a specific area of the STOCK EXCHANGE floor used for the trading of COMMODITIES, FUTURES and so on.

placing a method of raising new share capital by issuing shares in a company to a selected group of investors rather than to the public.

planned capital expenditure program a program of capital expenditure as set out in the corporate financial plan.

planned financing program a strategy for short and long-term financial planning as set out in the corporate financial plan.

planning blight the difficulty that is experienced in selling, leasing or developing a building or site owing to the fact that the building or site is affected by some kind of government or local authority projected development plan.

planning permission (Brit) the permission that in the UK has to be obtained from a local authority before changing a building or site in some way or before building on a site.

plant a large item of PHYSICAL CAPITAL used as equipment in the operation of the production part of a business.

plc *or* **PLC** the abbreviation for PUBLIC LIMITED COMPANY.

plowed-back profit *same as* RETAINED PROFIT.

point of sale the place where a consumer makes a purchase. This is usually a RETAIL shop.

point of sale display promotional material for a product displayed in the RETAIL OUTLET where the product is to be sold. Such material includes posters, banners and display units.

portfolio 1 a collection of FINANCIAL SECURITIES that is held by an investor. 2 a list of the loans made by an organization. 3 a collection of products that are marketed by a firm.

poison pill in a hostile takeover situation, any action taken by the TARGET COMPANY that will make it less attractive to the prospective buyer. See also TAKEOVER BID.

poison put in a hostile MERGER situation, an arrangement whereby a bondholder can demand repayment of the BOND if the merger goes ahead.

post in a STOCK EXCHANGE, that part of the floor where trading in STOCKS listed on the exchange takes place.

post-date to insert a date on a document that is later than the date on which the signing of the document takes place, the document being legally effective from the later date.

post-testing testing that is undertaken after the

appearance of an advertisement to try to establish whether the objectives set for it have been met.

pound 1 the standard monetary unit in the UK, made up of 100 pence. **2** the standard monetary unit of the Falkland Islands and Gibraltar. **3** the standard monetary unit of Egypt, Lebanon, the Sudan and Syria made up of 100 PIASTRES. **4** the standard monetary unit of Cyprus, made up of 100 cents.

power of attorney a legal instrument that allows one party to act on behalf of another party, either for a specific purpose or in general.

PR the abbreviation for PUBLIC RELATIONS.

pre-acquisition the RETAINED PROFIT of a company before its acquisition or TAKEOVER.

predatory pricing a pricing strategy that prices goods or services at such a low level that other firms are unable to compete and so get out of the market.

preference share a share in a company that pays a fixed rate of INTEREST rather than a variable DIVIDEND. In the event of the company going into LIQUIDATION, holders of preference shares are paid off before holders of ORDINARY SHARES after all debts have been discharged.

preliminary expenses the initial costs that are involved in a company. Such costs include the preparing of a PROSPECTUS and the issuing of shares.

premium 1 the payment made to an insurance company by a person or firm taking out insurance protection. *See* INSURANCE. **2** an amount that is in excess of the nominal value of a share, bond or other financial security. **3** an amount that is in excess of the ISSUE PRICE of a share or other financial security. **4** the price that is paid by the buyer of an OPTION contract to the seller for the right to exercise the option. **5** the difference in amount between the SPOT PRICE for a commodity or a currency and the FORWARD PRICE.

premium bond a BOND that sells for more than its PAR VALUE.

premium bonds (Brit) a FINANCIAL SECURITY issued by the UK government as a means of raising government revenue and as a means of encouraging members of the public to save. Premium bonds do not pay interest and no capital gain is offered but the bonds are entered in a regular draw, winners being drawn electronically by ERNIE (electronic random number indicating equipment).

prepackaged bankruptcy a BANKRUPTCY in which the CREDITORS of a failed company pre-arrange a strategy to deal with the bankruptcy, which is then filed with the bankruptcy petition.

president the top officer in an organization.

preventive maintenance a planned system of

maintenance that aims to minimize or eliminate breakdown in equipment and machinery by a program of regular inspection and repairs.

price competition competition between rival companies that is based on price.

price control a system of restrictions on prices of CONSUMER GOODS and services enforced by a government, usually in an attempt to control INFLATION.

price discrimination the practice of selling the same products at different prices to different buyers.

price index a method of showing the relative change in the price of a product between a given year and a base year. See CONSUMER PRICE INDEX.

prices and incomes policy an economic policy established by the government involving the imposition of controls both on wages and on prices in an effort to curb INFLATION.

price war fierce competition between two or more firms in the same industry, involving aggressive price cutting in an attempt to gain the largest share of the market.

primary market 1 the first buyer of a new SECURITY issue buys that security in the primary market. **2** the geographical area or a particular type of customer that constitutes the main market for a particular product or service.

prime costs *see* DIRECT COSTS.

prime rate the rate of INTEREST charged by banks to their best (prime) business customers, i.e. those with the highest CREDIT RATING.

principal 1 a sum of money on which INTEREST is earned. **2** a person for whom an AGENT or BROKER acts.

prior charges interest payments on DEBENTURES and loan stock that must be paid by a company before any of its shareholders can be paid dividend payments.

private enterprise an economic system in which individuals are encouraged to be entrepreneurs and to run their own businesses and make profits with the minimum of state involvement.

private ledger a ledger that contains confidential accounts and to which access is restricted to a few authorized personnel.

private limited company *see* LIMITED COMPANY, FLOTATION.

private placement the sale of a SECURITY privately to an exclusive group of investors.

private sector the section of a country's economy that is not under state control but is owned and run by private individuals or companies.

privatization the transference of a publicly owned company or industry from the state to the PRIVATE SECTOR. *See* NATIONALIZATION.

process-focused layout *or* **process-oriented layout** a factory or office layout in which all the production operations of a similar kind are grouped together in the same part of the factory or department. Process-focused layout is particularly appropriate in situations in which small quantities of a large range of products are to be manufactured, for example in small engineering workshops.

producer price index (Brit) an index in the UK that is a measure of the rate of INFLATION among goods manufactured and purchased, monitoring the movement in prices of about 10,000 goods with relevance to the same base year.

product 1 a name applied to both goods and services that are purchased by consumers. **2** an item that is manufactured by a company.

product costs the total costs of making a product, including DIRECT COSTS, comprising direct MATERIALS COSTS and direct LABOR COSTS, and INDIRECT COSTS or OVERHEADS.

product cycle the length of time needed to bring a new product to the commercial marketplace. *See also* PRODUCT LIFE CYCLE.

product development a business strategy undertaken by a company to increase sales and profitability. It consists of developing new or modified products for existing markets or promoting products in new markets.

product differentiation the means by which a supplier's

product is distinguished from a similar product made by a competitor. The products are differentiated by differences in appearance, such as design and color of packaging, and by the use of advertising and sales promotional techniques.

product diversification a business strategy undertaken by a company to increase sales and profitability and consisting of developing new products for new consumers or markets.

product-focused layout *or* **product-oriented layout** a factory or office layout in which the position of the work stations, equipment, etc, is arranged to suit the needs of the product, the machinery being arranged in the same order and sequence as the operations necessary for production of the product.

production the process that transforms materials, labor and capital into goods and services.

production cost center the part of an organization where production is carried out.

production line a method of production in which a product is manufactured by passing it through a number of operations, materials or components being added at the appropriate stages of operation.

productivity a measure of the output of a company per unit of input, often measured in terms of output per man hour.

productivity agreement an agreement reached between an employer and employees or between employers and unions by which an increase in wages is related to an increase in PRODUCTIVITY.

product liability the legal liability that manufacturers or others carry for defective products.

product life cycle the course of a product's life from its development and its introduction to the market to its eventual decline when demand falls or it is displaced by a new product. The cycle is usually considered to consist of the development stage, during which the original concept becomes a PROTOTYPE and marketing plans are put together; the introduction stage, when the product is launched on the market, when sales are likely to be low as consumers are unused to the product and when advertising measures and introductory offers might be used to help introduce the product to the public; the growth stage, when sales volume is likely to increase as the product becomes known to the consumer and demand increases and when competitors' versions of the product are likely to appear; the maturity stage, when sales and demand become equal, sales stabilize and further expansion of the market is difficult so that much emphasis is placed on advertising, sales promotion and price cuts; the decline stage, when sales fall to the stage when the supplier feels that it is best to withdraw the product from the market and concentrate on other products.

product line a group of closely related versions of a product, for example a number of versions of a particular make of car.

product portfolio a collection of products that are marketed by one company.

profit the difference that occurs when a company's sales revenue is greater than its total costs in providing the relevant goods or services, also being defined as the surplus of a company's NET ASSETS at the end of an ACCOUNTING PERIOD over the net assets at the beginning of that period.

profitability the potential of a product to make a profit or the capacity of a company to make a profit.

profit-and-loss account an accounting statement in the books of a company or organization that indicates the profits or losses that have been made on its business activities after the deduction of the relevant expenses.

profit margin the difference between the selling price of a product and the costs of producing and selling it.

profit-sharing a system by which a portion of the

profits of a company are distributed to the employees.

pro forma financial statement a financial statement that includes details of transactions that have not yet taken place.

pro forma invoice an invoice that is sometimes sent to a customer in advance of a transaction before some of the invoice details are known, a final invoice being sent when all the details are known.

pro forma statement a financial statement that includes projected future operating costs and results.

progressive tax a tax, such as INCOME TAX, that increases with increases in the base tax.

promissory note a document that contains a promise to pay a certain sum of money to a specified named person or to the bearer and must be delivered to the payee or bearer.

prompt day *or* **prompt date 1** the day or date on which payment becomes due for the purchase of goods. **2** the date on which a contract commodity exchange matures.

property bond a BOND that is issued by a life insurance company, the premiums for which are invested in a property-owning fund.

proposed dividend a DIVIDEND that has been recommended to be paid by the directors of a company but that has not yet been paid.

prospectus a document that sets out details about a NEW ISSUE of SHARES and invites the public to subscribe for the shares.

protectionism the measures that are sometimes taken by a country to protect certain of its domestic industries from competition from other countries' products.

prototype a preproduction model of a product that is being developed so that various features of it can be evaluated and modified in the finished product if necessary.

provision an amount that is allotted from PROFITS in a company's accounts either in respect of a known LIABILITY, although the exact amount of that might not be known, or in respect of the reduction in value of an ASSET.

proxy a person who acts as a representative of another person or firm, for example at the annual general meeting of a company at which the proxy may vote on behalf of the person or company that has nominated him or her, provided written authorization is given to the proxy. The word 'proxy' can also apply to the authorization to represent someone else in this way.

PSBR the abbreviation for PUBLIC SECTOR BORROWING REQUIREMENT.

public issue a method of issuing a NEW ISSUE of SHARES, loan stocks, etc, in which members of the public apply for shares at a fixed price, the company making the issue known to the public by advertisements in the press.

public limited company (Brit) (usually abbreviated to **plc** or **PLC**) a company that is registered as a public company under the Companies Act of 1980 and that may offer shares and securities to the public. The title of such companies must end with the initials plc.

public relations (often abbreviated to **PR**) a means of promoting a company in a favorable light to the public with a view to encouraging people to buy its products or invest in its shares. Larger companies often employ a public relations officer to liaise with the media and to provide handouts to the press about the company's activities and policies. Other companies employ a public relations company.

public sector borrowing requirement (often abbreviated to **PSBR**) the amount of money that the government requires to borrow in order to make up for a budget deficit.

pul an Afghan monetary unit, equal to one hundredth of an AFGHANI.

pula the standard monetary unit of Botswana, made up of 100 thebes.

pump priming the injection of money into the economy by the government in the form of, for example, major public works.

punt the former standard monetary unit of the Republic of Ireland, made up of 100 pence, replaced by the Euro on January 1 2002..

purchase ledger the LEDGER in which are recorded the personal accounts of a company's suppliers.

pya a monetary unit of Myanmar (Burma), worth one hundredth of a KYAT.

pyramid scheme a fraudulent scheme in which an unscrupulous person persuades others to invest in his or her business by promising a very high RETURN. He or she then uses the money paid by these new investors to pay off any other investors who insist on having their money back – or just keeps the money for himself or herself. Pyramid schemes are illegal.

Q

qindar *see* LEK.

qualitative analysis an evaluation that measures factors that are difficult to assess, such as staff morale. *See also* QUANTITATIVE ANALYSIS.

quality control the process of ascertaining that the quality of a product or service meets specified performance criteria that will ensure a high standard of product or service. *See also* ACCEPTANCE SAMPLING.

quango (Brit) an acronym for **quasi-autonomous non-governmental organization** an executive body that, although not a government agency as such, is often ultimately responsible to a government minister and is appointed to oversee a specified area of public-sector activity and expenditure.

quantitative analysis an evaluation that measures factors that are easy to assess, such as production costs. *See also* QUALITATIVE ANALYSIS.

quantity discount a price reduction to buyers who purchase a product in large quantities.

quasi-contract an obligation that one party is deemed by a court to have to another, although there is no formal contract between the parties. For example, if an overpayment is made to someone by mistake, that person is obliged to repay the money.

quetzal the standard monetary unit of Guatemala, made up of 100 CENTAVOS.

quick assets ASSETS that can be quickly converted into cash.

quick ratio a measure of a company's financial strength. It is worked out by taking CURRENT ASSETS (minus inventories) divided by CURRENT LIABILITIES. Also known as the Acid Test ratio.

quota a restriction on the trade in, or in the production of, a particular product imposed, for example, by a government or supplier.

quotation 1 the price and terms on which a tradesman, company, etc, is prepared to provide a service or goods. **2** the official price of a SECURITY or COMMODITY. **3** permission from the regulatory authority of a stock market for the shares of a company to be traded in that market.

quoted company *same as* LISTED COMPANY

R

Racketeer Influenced and Corrupt Organizations Act (RICO) a Federal law intended to prevent INSIDER TRADING.

raider an individual or organization that makes a habit of initiating hostile TAKEOVER BIDS, having identified suitable companies with undervalued assets.

rally in the STOCK MARKET, a rise in prices after a fall. *See also* REACTION.

rand the standard monetary unit of South Africa and Namibia, being made up of 100 cents.

R & D the abbreviated form of RESEARCH AND DEVELOPMENT.

rate of exchange the price of one country's currency in terms of the price of another, for example, the number of US dollars that will be received in return for a pound sterling. Two rates of exchange are usually quoted by banks, etc – the buying and the selling rate. The difference between the two takes account of the profit or commission charged by the organization that is carrying out the exchange.

rate of return the annual amount of INCOME that is derived from an INVESTMENT. This is often expressed as a percentage of the original investment.

rationalization the reorganization of an organization or industry with the intention of increasing efficiency and profitability.

raw materials basic materials that are converted into finished products or components of finished products. Examples of raw materials include wood, iron ore and wool.

RD *or* **rd** the abbreviated form of REFER TO DRAWER.

reaction in the STOCK MARKET, a fall in prices after a rise. *See also* RALLY.

real assets ASSETS such as buildings and equipment that are easily identifiable.

real capital financial ASSETS such as savings and REAL ESTATE.

real estate land or anything fixed to it, such as a building, fence or tree, and anything beneath the surface, such as oil.

real exchange rates exchange rates that have been calculated to take account of the different levels of INFLATION between two countries.

realtor a person who acts as an agent for people buying or selling REAL ESTATE.

real interest rate the actual INTEREST rate less whatever the current rate of INFLATION is standing at.

recall test a test that is used in advertising research to try to establish how well people can remember the details of an advertisement that they have seen.

receivership (Brit) a situation in which a company defaults on a DEBT or debts and a **receiver** is appointed to realize the company's ASSETS in order to pay off any creditors, such as those who hold a MORTGAGE or charge over a company's property.

recession a fall or marked slowing-down in the rate of growth of the GROSS DOMESTIC PRODUCT. It is usually associated with a marked rise in the unemployment rate and with a fall in property prices.

recovery the period after a RECESSION during which the economy starts to improve. It is characterized by a slow increase in consumer spending and a decrease in unemployment.

recovery stock stock that has fallen in value but is thought to have the potential to recover its original value.

redeemable shares shares that the issuing company has the right to redeem under certain terms that are stipulated when the shares are issued.

redemption redeeming or paying off a LOAN.

redemption date the date on which a redeemable FINANCIAL SECURITY has to be repaid.

redemption value the worth of a BOND or other investment at a specific time or on maturity.

rediscounting the discounting of a BILL OF

EXCHANGE or BOND that has already been discounted, usually by a DISCOUNT HOUSE.

re-exports goods that have been imported and then exported again without having been subjected to any process while in the country that imported them. *See* ENTREPOT TRADE.

refer to drawer (Brit) (often abbreviated to **RD** *or* **rd**) a phrase written on a check to indicate that a bank is not going to honor it. This is usually because there is insufficient money in the account of the person who has written the check to cover the value of the check and because the bank is unwilling to allow the account to go into (further) OVERDRAFT. Sometimes there are other reasons, such as that the person who has written the check has stopped it or because there is an inaccuracy in the check, such as the wrong date or a missing signature.

refinancing the process of repaying part or all of the LOAN CAPITAL of a company by acquiring new loans, the latter usually having been negotiated at a lower rate of interest than the original loan capital.

reflation a government fiscal or government policy that is aimed at expanding the output of the economy. This could involve the increase of the available money supply, increasing government expenditure on investment and public works or the reduction of taxation and interest rates.

regional fund a MUTUAL FUND that invests in a specific area abroad.

registered check a CHECK issued by a bank on behalf of a client who has reserved sufficient funds to cover the check.

registered company (Brit) a company registered under the COMPANIES ACT. Such a company has to be registered with the REGISTRAR OF COMPANIES.

registered name (Brit) the name under which a company is registered in the United Kingdom.

registered office (Brit) the official address of a company in the United Kingdom to which all official correspondence must be sent.

registered trademark a legally protected design which distinguishes a product from its competitors. A registered trademark is signified by a ® symbol.

registered trader a member of a STOCK EXCHANGE who trades in particular STOCKS on his or her own account.

register of charges 1 a list of the charges on its assets that a company must keep. This is lodged at its REGISTERED OFFICE or its head office and is the responsibility of the company registrar. The register of charges must be made available for inspection by shareholders, creditors and others during normal office business hours. **2** a register that is kept by the REGISTRAR OF COMPANIES on which companies must register certain charges against its assets of the kind set out in the COMPANIES ACT.

register of members (Brit) a list of the shareholders of a company that must be kept at the company's REGISTERED OFFICE or head office.

registrar a financial institution appointed to record all transactions regarding the issue and ownership of a company's securities. *See* SECURITY.

Registrar of Companies (Brit) a government official who is responsible for maintaining a record of companies that operate in the United Kingdom and for undertaking duties connected with the registering of companies, such as issuing incorporation certificates and receiving copies of annual returns that companies have to send in, these being subject to inspection by anyone who requires information on the background of a particular company.

registration statement a rule set out in the Federal Securities Act of 1933, that a company issuing new securities must file full details about the firm and the SECURITY issue involved.

regressive tax a form of tax in which the rate of tax, such as INDIRECT TAX, decreases as income increases.

relative strength the price movement of a STOCK as

compared to the general movement of the STOCK MARKET.

relaunch the reintroduction of a product or service into a market after some alterations have been made to it to increase its market appeal.

relocation the transference from one place of work to another. The term can refer to a company that is moving from one place to another as a result of MERGER, TAKEOVER BID, etc, or to a worker who is moving from one area to another because of work opportunities.

Rembrandt market the foreign market in the Netherlands.

remuneration money paid in the form of wages, salary or fees for work done or services rendered.

renewal notice a communication from an insurance company inviting a policy-holder to renew the policy when it is about to expire.

renunciation the surrender to someone else of shares offered to someone in a RIGHTS ISSUE.

reorder level a pre-arranged level to which stocks of a product must drop before an order for more of the product is placed.

replacement-chain problem the necessity of taking into account the need to replace ASSETS when making financial calculations about possible future projects.

replacement cost the cost of replacing a FIXED ASSET

or item of stock, either in its present form or in an equivalent form.

replacement cycle the frequency with which an ASSET, such as a piece of machinery, must be replaced.

replacement price the current market cost of an item. The replacement price is usually higher than the original purchase price.

replacement value the cost of replacing a firm's ASSETS.

repo in the STOCK MARKET, an agreement between two parties in which the first party sells a SECURITY to the second party and agrees to buy it back on a certain date at a certain price.

reporting currency the currency in which a firm prepares its financial statements. For a US company, this would be in US dollars.

repositioning the altering of the design, packaging, BRAND NAME, BRAND IMAGE, etc, of a product in order to change its position in the market in relation to its competitors as perceived by consumers.

repossession the process of taking back something that is being paid for by installments or by a MORTGAGE system when the contracted regular payments have not been met.

repurchase agreement *see* REPO.

resale price maintenance where a manufacturer

fixes the minimum price for which their goods may be sold to retail customers.

rescission cancellation. After rescission of a CONTRACT, the parties return to the same condition they were in prior to the making of the contract.

research and development (often abbreviated to **R & D**) the department of a company and the portion of its resources that are concerned with research into potential new products and the process of modification of such research aimed at their ultimate development as commercially viable products.

reserve price the lowest price that a seller is willing to accept for an article offered for sale to the public at auction.

restrictive trade practices agreements between traders relating to restrictions on prices, terms, conditions of sale, etc, which are not held to be in the interests of the public and may be detrimental to other suppliers.

retailer an individual or company that stocks a particular type of product or a range of products for sale to consumers, as opposed to a WHOLESALER.

retail outlet business premises where products are sold to consumers.

retained profit the amount of profit that remains after tax has been deducted and after dividends have been paid to shareholders and is reinvested in the company.

retrenchment reducing the expenses of running a business, such as cutting back on personnel, usually in an effort to save money.

return the income derived from an investment, which is frequently expressed as a percentage of its original cost.

revenue 1 cash received from the sale of products or services. **2** earnings.

revenue expenditure any expenditure that is written off entirely in the PROFIT-AND-LOSS ACCOUNT in the financial year to which it is relevant.

reverse takeover 1 a TAKEOVER by a company that has a lower stock valuation than the firm that is the object of the takeover. **2** the takeover of a public company by a private company.

revocable trust a trust that can be ended by its founder.

rial 1 the standard monetary unit of Iran, made up of 100 DINARS. **2** the standard monetary unit of Oman, made up of 100 BAIZAS.

rider a clause added to a CONTRACT, insurance policy etc, that modifies some aspect of the original document.

riel the standard monetary unit of Cambodia, made up of 100 SEN.

rights issue a method by which companies raise new CAPITAL by the issue of new SHARES. Existing shareholders are offered new shares in proportion to the number of shares that they already hold, usually at a price below the current market price. The existing shareholders who do not wish to subscribe to the extra shares can sell their rights on the market.

ring a number of manufacturers, suppliers or traders who make an agreement, often an illegal agreement, to further their own interests by controlling the price of a product or its conditions of sale in a way that is beneficial to them.

ringgit *see* SEN.

risk the element of uncertainty on the return of an ASSET; the possibility of experiencing harm or loss.

risk analysis the process of studying an investment or a possible course of action to evaluate potential risks and put in place techniques to minimize the effects of these. Also known as risk management.

risk averse an investor who prefers low risk investments.

risk capital any business CAPITAL that is invested in a project when there is a significant element of risk of loss in the event of the project failing.

risk free investment an investment, such as a US Treasury bill, where the future RETURN is known from the beginning.

risk free rate the rate earned on a RISK FREE INVEST-MENT.

riskless rate the INTEREST RATE received from a RISK FREE INVESTMENT, such as a US Treasury bill.

risk lover an investor who will accept investments with higher than normal amounts of RISK.

risk management see RISK ANALYSIS.

risk neutral an investor who does not care one way or the other about the level of RISK involved in a specific investment.

risk premium an additional return on an investment that is given to an investor in order to compensate him or her for the possibility of losing the investment in the event of the project failing.

risky asset an ASSET on which the future RETURN is unknown.

riyal 1 the standard monetary unit of Saudi Arabia, made up of 100 HALALA. **2** the standard monetary unit of Qatar, made up of 100 DIRHAMS. **3** the standard monetary unit of Yemen, made up of 100 FILS.

Romalpa clause a clause in a contract of sale by which the seller of the goods retains the right to their ownership until the goods have been paid for.

rouble the standard monetary unit of Russia, Belarus and Tajikistan, made up of 100 kopeks.

round lot in the STOCK MARKET, a trade of 100

shares of a particular STOCK (or multiples of 100). *See also* ODD LOT.

route sheet *or* **routing sheet** a document that shows in detail the sequence of operations through which a product or component passes and often the tools and equipment required. When this is computerized, it makes it particularly easy to track down a particular point in a process.

royalties payments paid for the right to make use of property belonging to someone else for one's own gain. This property may take the form of physical property, such as a mine or quarry, in which case royalties are paid on the right to make use of these for extracting minerals, etc, or it may take the form of INTELLECTUAL PROPERTY, such as the COPYRIGHT of a book or an invention PATENT.

rubber check (slang) a check that is worthless because it is drawn on an account with insufficient funds.

rufiyaa the standard monetary unit of the Maldives, made up of 100 LAARI.

running costs the costs that are incurred in the operation of a company or FIXED ASSET, such as expenditure on power in a factory and that on gas, servicing etc on a motor vehicle.

rupee 1 the standard monetary unit of India, Pakistan and Nepal, made up of 100 PAISA. **2** the standard monetary unit of Sri Lanka, Mauritius and the Seychelles, made up of 100 cents.

rupiah the standard monetary unit of Indonesia, made up of 100 SEN.

Rust Belt, Rust Bowl a reference to the eastern seaboard area of the US, formerly known as the Steel Belt, and now largely abandoned.

S

salary payment, usually paid monthly and usually expressed as an annual amount, made by employers to employees in return for work done.

sale and leaseback an agreement by which the owner of an ASSET sells it to a purchaser and immediately purchases from the new owner the right to use the asset under a LEASE arrangement.

sale and repurchase agreement an agreement by which the owner of an asset sells it to a purchaser on condition that the original owner is allowed to repurchase the asset under certain circumstances.

sale as seen a selling process in which the purchaser inspects the goods before the purchase and carries out the purchase solely on the basis of this inspection rather than on the basis of any guarantee of quality by the seller.

sale or return a selling process in which a seller agrees to take back from the purchaser, either a consumer or a retailer, any goods that remain unused or unsold, usually within a certain period of time.

sales analysis a detailed survey of the information

relating to a company's sales in order to evaluate the efficiency and profitability of this and to identify anything that can be done to improve this.

sales forecasting the process by which a company tries to estimate the likely volume of future sales and the extent of future sales revenue, taking into consideration past trends and any information relating to current or future marketing circumstances, such as economic forecasts, government regulations, etc.

sales invoice a document that is sent by a seller of goods or services to the purchaser indicating the amount of payment due.

sales ledger a company ledger that records the personal accounts of the company's customers, the total of the balances in this register representing the company's trade debtors.

sales presentation a formal demonstration where a company's representative presents the benefits of a product or service to a potential customer, answers questions and queries and does his or her best to make a sale.

sales promotion a process that is designed to increase the sales of a company's goods or services, including advertising campaigns and materials, public relations activity, temporary price reductions, free samples or gifts, etc.

sales quota a target that is set by the management of a company for its sales representatives.

sales tax a tax that is imposed at the point of sale.

salvage value the scrap value of a firm's equipment.

Samurai bond a BOND issued in Tokyo, denominated in yen, by a non-Japanese borrower. See also BULLDOG BOND, YANKEE BOND.

Samurai market the foreign market in Japan.

sandbag tactics tactics adopted by the management of a company that is the unwilling target of a TAKEOVER BID, such tactics including protracted talks with the unwanted bidder to gain time to see if a more welcome solution such as a suitable WHITE KNIGHT can be found. See also BLACK KNIGHT, GRAY KNIGHT, YELLOW KNIGHT.

santim *see* LATS.

satang a monetary unit of Thailand, equal to one hundredth of a BAHT.

Saturday night special STOCK MARKET slang for a sudden and unexpected TAKEOVER BID, often announced over a weekend, when the stock markets are closed, so as to avoid publicity.

savings account an account in a bank or SAVINGS AND LOAN ASSOCIATION into which personal savings are paid, usually attracting a higher rate of interest than a DEPOSIT ACCOUNT and usually involving some kind of restriction on withdrawals.

savings and loan association an organization, chartered by the Federal or state government, that uses the savings of its members to finance long-term LOANS, especially MORTGAGES.

savings bond a bond specifically aimed at small investors and individuals, issued by the US Treasury Department and widely available at outlets such as post offices and banks.

Say's Law of Markets a theory, put forward by the French economist Jean Baptiste Say, that supply creates its own demand.

SBIC abbreviation for Small Business Investment Company.

scalp STOCK MARKET slang meaning to trade for very low gains.

scalper one who acquires, then sells on, tickets for a popular event for as much money as he or she can get, sometimes for many times their face value.

Schilling the former standard monetary unit of Austria, made up of 100 GROSCHEN, replaced by the Euro on January 1 2002.

scrip issue the issue of new share certificates to existing SHAREHOLDERS without any further CAPITAL being required to be paid. Such issues are usually made when a company has accumulated substantial reserves after plowing back profits into the business over several years or after revaluing its FIXED ASSETS and accumulated CAPITAL RESERVES.

seasonal fluctuation the influence of the seasons on some kinds of business activities. For example sales of ice cream and cold drinks is highest in the summer months.

SEC *see* SECURITIES AND EXCHANGE COMMISSION.

second mortgage a MORTGAGE taken out on a property that is already mortgaged in order to raise LOAN CAPITAL.

Securities and Exchange Commission (SEC) created in 1934, the SEC is a Federal agency that supervises the US financial markets.

security 1 an ASSET or group of assets to which a lender of money has recourse if the borrower of the money DEFAULTS on the agreed loan repayments, the security often being referred to as COLLATERAL, particularly in the case of banks. **2** a financial asset such as a SHARE, BOND or STOCK.

seed capital a small amount of CAPITAL that is needed to pay for any research and development that has to be carried out before the setting up of a new business.

self-assessment a taxation system by which taxpayers assess their own INCOME TAX liabilities and CAPITAL GAINS liabilities for the tax year.

self-financing referring to a company that is able to fund its capital expenditure from its undistributed profits rather than from loans.

self-liquidating 1 referring to a LOAN in which the money loaned is used to fund a project that is expected to yield enough money to repay the loan and any INTEREST payable on the loan and leave a profit. **2** referring to an ASSET that earns back its original cost out of income over a set period of time. **3** referring to a SALES PROMOTION offer that is expected to make enough money in increased sales to pay for the money spent on the offer.

seller's market a market situation in which the demand for goods, services or securities is greater than the supply and which thus enables sellers to increase prices.

sen 1 a monetary unit of Cambodia, equal to one hundredth of a RIEL. **2** a monetary unit of Malaysia, equal to one hundredth of a ringgit. **3** a former monetary unit of Japan, equal to one hundredth of a yen. It is still used as a unit of account.

sene a monetary unit of Western Samoa, equal to one hundredth of a tala.

seniti a monetary unit of Tonga, equal to one hundredth of a PA'ANGA.

separation a euphemism for the dismissal, retirement or resignation of an employee. Also known as TERMINATION.

sequestration the confiscation of the property of a person or organization because of failure to comply with a court order.

service an economic activity that is carried out to meet a personal or business demand. Unlike the provision of goods, the provision of services does not result in the transfer of ownership of any tangible object. Services cover many fields and include such activities as hairdressing, window-cleaning, machine maintenance, dentistry, accountancy and banking.

service contract a contract of employment between an employer and employee, usually a senior employee such as a manager or director, that sets out the terms and conditions of employment.

service industry the section of industry that is concerned with the provision of a SERVICE rather than goods.

settlement 1 the payment of an outstanding DEBT or LOAN. **2** the conclusion of an INDUSTRIAL DISPUTE or civil litigation as a result of a voluntary agreement between the parties involved.

settlement date the date on which payment must be made to conclude an agreement.

set-up time the time that is taken in setting up a machine or operation to carry out a production task, it being the aim of a company to minimize this unproductive time.

share a FINANCIAL SECURITY that is issued by a company as a means of raising long-term CAPITAL, the share being one of a number of titles of ownership in a company and conferring on the holder a legal right to part of the profits of a company, usually paid in the form of DIVIDENDS, and often voting rights. *See* ORDINARY SHARE and PREFERENCE SHARE.

share capital the part of the CAPITAL of a company that derives from the issue of SHARES.

share certificate a document that is issued to provide evidence of the ownership of shares in a company.

share-for-share offer a form of TAKEOVER BID in which the directors of the company seeking to make such a bid for another company offer shares in their own company in payment for shares in the TARGET COMPANY.

shareholder a person who owns SHARES in a company.

share issue the process of issuing SHARES in a company.

share option 1 an offer sometimes offered to employees of a company under which they are given the option to buy shares in the company at a favorable price. **2** *see* OPTION.

share premium the amount of money paid for shares issued by a company, the price of which is higher than the nominal value of the shares.

share register a record of the shareholders of a company, which lists the names and addresses of the SHAREHOLDERS, the extent of their shareholding and the class of SHARES that they hold, this record constituting evidence of ownership. The relevant officer is legally obliged to maintain an up-to-date share register.

share shop (Brit) a financial intermediary, such as a stockbroker or bank officer, who is appointed by the government to deal with applications for SHARES issued in connection with the PRIVATIZATION of an organization, with a view to attracting members of the public who are not usually in the habit of buying shares and who do not know how to go about doing so.

share split the division of the SHARE CAPITAL into smaller units, in which the number of shares is increased and the nominal value of the SHARES is reduced. A share split usually takes place when the share prices in a company reach such a high value that trading in them causes problems.

share warehousing the practice of accumulating a holding of the SHARES in a company that is the target of a TAKEOVER BID, the shares being gradually bought in the name of several nominees and kept until the prospective takeover bidder has built up a significant number of shares in the TARGET COMPANY.

share warrant a document that gives the holder

the right to buy a security at a particular price at a particular date in the future.

shark an unscrupulous business person, especially one who tries to take over a business against the wishes of its owners. See TAKEOVER BID.

shark repellent an alteration to a company's charter that will make it less attractive to a possible hostile TAKEOVER BID; a type of POISON PILL.

shell company 1 a company that is no longer trading but may have a listing on the STOCK EXCHANGE and may be used for various company maneuvers. For example, a shell company may be the target of a TAKEOVER BID by a company that is not itself listed on the stock exchange. **2** a company that has ceased to trade and that is sold to new owners for a small fee, the object being to save the cost and trouble of setting up a new business.

shequel the standard monetary unit of Israel, equal to 100 agorot.

shilling the standard monetary unit of Kenya, Somalia, Tanzania and Uganda, equal to 100 cents.

Shogun bond a BOND, denominated in US dollars, issued in Japan by a non-resident. *See also* SAMURAI BOND.

shop WALL STREET jargon for a firm.

shop floor a name given to the basic level in a company at which are produced the goods or services that are the basis of the company's business activity, for example, the operatives producing components or finished goods in a factory.

shopping in the STOCK MARKET, contacting a number of dealers or BROKERS to try and obtain the best price available for a trade.

shop steward (Brit) an employee of a company who represents the interests of his or her colleagues in negotiations with management, often being the representative of the LABOR UNION of which the company employees are members.

short bill a BILL OF EXCHANGE that is payable within a very short time, either on demand, at sight or within ten days.

short-dated gilts *or* **shorts** GILT-EDGED SECURITIES that are redeemable in less than five years.

shortfall a shortage of CASH or INCOME; less cash or income than was expected in a particular period.

short position a situation in which a dealer or MARKET MAKER in a particular SECURITY, COMMODITY or foreign currency is selling more than he or she is buying or holding in expectation of prices falling.

shorts *see* SHORT-DATED GILTS.

short-term credit CREDIT extending for a period of up to one year. Short-term credit often has lower INTEREST RATES than long-term credit.

short-term financial plan a financial plan covering the coming FISCAL YEAR only.

short-term financing a LOAN that must be repaid within the year.

shrinkage a term given to goods that are no longer in a retail outlet but have not been recorded as having been sold. Goods in this category may have been stolen, broken, damaged or have been disposed of because they have passed their sell-by date.

sight deposit a bank deposit that can be withdrawn on demand without notice.

sight draft a BILL OF EXCHANGE that is payable on sight, no matter when it was drawn.

Siliconaires (slang) a reference to the young entrepreneurs behind the dotcom boom of the late 1990s, who suddenly found themselves extremely wealthy thanks to their STOCK holdings in SILICON VALLEY internet companies.

Silicon Valley the region in Northern California known for its large number of computer and internet companies.

silver parachute a severance package offered to employees when a company is taken over. See also GOLDEN PARACHUTE.

simplified financial statements simplified versions of the annual accounts of a company prepared for readers, such as workers or shareholders, who do not possess specialist financial knowledge and who might not otherwise understand the accounts.

sinful stock STOCK from organizations that are perceived to be associated in some way with activities that some may see as immoral or unethical. For example, companies involved in the arms trade, tobacco, alcohol and so on.

single currency a unified currency proposed for the use of all member states of the EUROPEAN UNION when economic and monetary union takes place.

single market an association of countries trading without restrictions, especially the countries of the EUROPEAN UNION.

sit-down strike a form of INDUSTRIAL ACTION in which the workers arrive at their place of work but refuse either to work or to leave the workplace.

skimming taking or hiding money. Skimming from a business is illegal.

slander an oral statement that defames the character of another. *See also* LIBEL.

sleeping beauty a company that presents an attractive opportunity for a TAKEOVER BID, but has not yet been approached.

sleeping partner a person who has CAPITAL in a business PARTNERSHIP and shares in the profits but who does not take any part in the business activity of the partnership.

slush fund an amount of money set aside for a non-designated purpose. Slush funds may, or may not, be used for illegal purposes, such as a political bribe.

smart money money that is invested by people who are experienced in and knowledgeable about money matters, especially when they have some inside information about a particular investment opportunity.

smurf (slang) referring to someone who is known to be involved in money LAUNDERING.

social audit a survey of the non-financial aspects of a company's performance, the object being to enable the company to assess its performance in relation to society. These aspects include the effect on the environment of the company's activities, the impact of the company on the local community and the wider public and its responsiveness to certain social issues such as equal opportunities.

social responsibility the idea that businesses should not only aim at maximizing their profits, but should also contribute something positive to society. Sponsoring educational and arts programs and reducing pollution are examples of corporate social responsibility schemes.

societal marketing a form of marketing that seeks

to meet the needs of consumers without damaging the environment or wasting natural resources.

socio-economic groups potential consumers grouped together in terms of certain social or economic considerations, such considerations including the type of employment. Such groups are used as the basis of identifying MARKET SEGMENTS, since the groups are likely to differ in the level and pattern of spending.

soft currency a currency that is known to experience marked fluctuations in value. An unstable currency. *See also* HARD CURRENCY.

soft loan a loan that has an INTEREST RATE charge that is much lower than the market rate of interest.

soft sell the use of gentle, low-key methods as an approach to selling, as opposed to the forceful methods of HARD SELL.

sole proprietorship indicates a business enterprise owned and operated by one person. In a sole proprietorship, the owner takes all the RISKS but also takes all the PROFITS.

solo a single BILL OF EXCHANGE of which no other copies are in circulation.

som the standard monetary unit of Kyrgyzstan.

source and application/uses of funds an accounting statement that indicates the sources from which a company has derived its funds and the uses to which these funds have been put during a specified trading period.

special deposits (Brit) deposits that the UK government may ask the CLEARING BANKS to place with the Bank of England as a means of controlling the money supply in the country, the point being that the less money the clearing banks hold, the less they will be able to lend to businesses.

specie money in the form of coins rather than in the form of bank notes or bullion.

speculation the purchase or sale of something with the sole purpose of making a CAPITAL profit. Professional speculation often takes place in the buying and selling of COMMODITIES, SECURITIES and foreign currencies, the prices of which are characterized by fluctuation, thereby giving those involved in speculation opportunities to make profits.

split-capital investment trust a kind of investment trust that has a limited life, the EQUITY capital being split into various classes of income shares and capital shares. The holders of income shares receive all or most of the income earned plus a preset amount of capital on LIQUIDATION, while holders of capital shares receive hardly any or no income but receive all the assets that remain after the income shares have been paid.

sponsor the issuing house that handles a NEW IS-SUE of SHARES for a company.

spot market a market that makes provision for the buying and selling of SECURITIES, COMMODITIES or foreign currencies for immediate delivery.

spot month the month in which goods bought on the basis of a FUTURES contract will become available for delivery.

spot price the current market price of a COMMODITY.

spread 1 the difference between the bid price, or buying price, and the offer price, or selling price, of a SECURITY, COMMODITY or foreign currency, which is quoted or made by a MARKET MAKER or dealer. **2** the simultaneous buying and selling of commodity FUTURES, the hope being that there will be some movement in the relative prices that will result in a profit.

spreadsheet in accounting, a computer program that arranges and links figures on screen in tables, rows and columns, thus allowing for automatic calculation and adjustment.

squeeze financial control imposed by a government to try to restrict INFLATION. Such a squeeze can be imposed, for example, on pay or on credit.

stag a person who applies for a large number of SHARES in a new share issue in the hope that the demand for the new shares will be in excess of the supply of the shares and that this will lead to an increase in the price of the shares when trading begins.

stagflation a period in the economy where there is high unemployment, rising prices and slow growth.

stakeholder a person who has an interest in the operation and performance of a company. Stakeholders include not only SHAREHOLDERS of the company but the company's employees, the company's customers and suppliers and the community in general, the latter's interest including the effect on the environment by the company.

stale check a check dated 90 to 180 days before being presented for payment. It will be marked as such and return unpaid to the party from whom it was received.

standard cost an estimated product cost that indicates in advance of production what a product ought to cost on the basis of reasonably efficient operations.

standard rate the average rate of work at which someone with the appropriate skills and motivation performs a task in the workplace.

standard time the time that it should take for someone with the required skills and motivation to complete a task in the workplace, taking account of time taken up by rest breaks, routine interruptions, machine breakdowns, etc.

starch test a method of measuring the effect of a printed advertisement on a potential customer by testing how much the consumer remembers about that particular ad.

statement of account a document, sent periodically by a company to a customer, that records the nature and value of the products that have been supplied and also records any amounts of money that are still owed.

statute a law passed by a legislative body.

statute of limitations a law that makes certain actions legally unenforceable after a certain period of time.

statutory voting the voting system in a corporation, where every share owned gives the holder one vote. Thus the more shares owned, the more power the shareholder enjoys.

sterling the name given to the UK POUND, mostly to distinguish it from the pound used as a monetary unit in other currencies.

stock 1 one or more SHARES in a corporation. **2** inventory, such as raw materials or goods ready for sale.

stock appreciation the amount by which the STOCK-IN-TRADE of a company has increased over a given period, perhaps because of INFLATION.

stockbroker an agent who acts as a market intermediary and buys and sells SECURITIES on a stock exchange on behalf of clients in return for remuneration in the form of commission.

stock control the process of regulating the STOCK-IN-TRADE of a company so that there is an adequate level maintained to meet requirements but the level is not unnecessarily high. This avoids large sums of money being tied up in it that could be used for other thing, and prevents money being wasted in warehousing it.

stock depreciation the amount by which the STOCK-IN-TRADE of a company has decreased over a given period of time, perhaps because of fluctuations in the market.

stock exchange *or* **stock market** a market in which SECURITIES are bought and sold, prices on the stock exchange being controlled by the forces of supply and demand. A stock market is used by public companies and governments to raise CAPITAL by selling securities to investors and is used by investors to sell their securities to others or to buy other securities from others.

stock-in-trade 1 the goods that a company has for the purpose of carrying out its business activities. Such goods include not only finished products but raw materials, components and WORK-IN-PROGRESS. **2** the goods or services that a company offers for sale.

stock market *same as* STOCK EXCHANGE.

stockpiling the accumulation and holding of levels of something, such as raw materials, food, etc, that are much higher than would be required in the course of normal use, in anticipation of a coming or expected shortage, price increase, etc.

stocktaking the process of counting and evaluating the physical amount of STOCK-IN-TRADE in a company and often checking it against the company records to ascertain what should be there. Stocktaking is usually undertaken in a company at least once a year in order to obtain a valuation of the stock-in-trade for the preparation of the company accounts.

stock valuation the setting of a money value on the various components of a firm's STOCK-IN-TRADE.

stock watering the creation of more SHARES by a company than is justifiable by the value of the company's TANGIBLE ASSETS, even although this may seem justified by the fact that the company is making considerable profits.

stores record card a record that is kept by a company for each item of STOCK-IN-TRADE, indicating the amount held, the amount received and issued and the stock that has been reserved to meet current orders.

stotin *see* TOLAR.

stotinka a monetary unit of Bulgaria, equal to one hundredth of a lev.

strap a triple OPTION on a security or commodity

market, consisting of one 'put' option and two 'call' options at the same price and for the same period. *See* STRIP.

strategic alliance a pooling of the resources and skills of two or more companies to enable them to engage effectively in a business activity, the firms involved continuing to operate separately in all other respects.

strategic fit the extent to which a new area of business activity in a company will fit with the current business activities of the company or what has been seen as its future scope.

strategic group a group of companies within a market or within an industry in which each company pursues broadly similar policies in relation to product, pricing, etc. Strategic-group analysis can be used to give valuable market information, such as the identification of possible gaps in the market and the identification of competitive advantages over a rival.

Street a reference to WALL STREET; includes brokers, dealers and other professional members of the financial community based in and around Wall Street.

strengths, weaknesses, opportunities and threats *see* SWOT ANALYSIS.

strike a form of INDUSTRIAL ACTION in which there is an organized refusal to work on the part of a workforce or on the part of some of the members of the workforce in order to force the employers to agree to the workers' demands, such as for higher pay, better working conditions, etc. A strike that is authorized and backed by a LABOR UNION is known as an **authorized strike**, while a strike that occurs without labor union authorization or backing is an **unauthorized strike**.

strip a triple OPTION on a security or commodity market, consisting of one 'call' option and two 'put' options at the same price and for the same period. *See* STRIP.

sub-agent a person or company employed to buy and sell goods on behalf of an AGENT, thus being the agent of an agent.

subordinated debt a DEBT that can be claimed by an unsecured CREDITOR on the liquidation of a company only after the claims of secured creditors have been met.

subpoena a summons to appear in a court. It is issued by a legal authority and requires someone to appear at a certain place at a specified time or face a penalty. See also SUMMONS.

subrogation the right of an insurer to take over any other methods that the insured person may have recourse to for acquiring compensation for the same occurrence, after the insured person has received any compensation due by the insurer. For example, an insurance company may pay for damage to a property caused by a known party and then take over the insured person's legal right to claim the cost of the repair from the person who caused it.

subscriber a person who agrees to pay for and receive a product, such as a magazine, for a specified period of time.

subscription shares the SHARES bought by the initial subscribers to a company.

subsidiary company a company that is owned by another company, known as the HOLDING COMPANY.

subsidy a payment paid by a government or organization to enable a certain business activity to take place or to take place more effectively or cheaply. Thus a government might pay a subsidy to a domestic industry to enable it to compete with foreign producers in the same industry.

sucre the standard monetary unit of Ecuador, equal to 100 CENTAVOS.

sum the standard monetary unit of Uzbekistan.

summary financial statement a shortened version of a company's annual accounts and report that is sometimes sent to shareholders instead of the full version.

summons a written instruction for a person to go to court. See also SUBPOENA.

Sun Belt a reference to the southern states of the USA.

sunk capital the value of a company's funds no longer available to that company because the money has been spent on ASSETS that are useless or unrealizable.

sunk costs the cost of durable items paid for by a company when these items can be treated as assets in the account books, although their value is unlikely to be recovered and cannot be used for any other purpose.

sunrise industries STOCK MARKET slang for emerging industries that are expected to dominate the market in future. See also SUNSET INDUSTRIES.

sunset industries declining industries. *See also* SUNRISE INDUSTRIES, RUST BELT.

superannuation an OCCUPATIONAL PENSION scheme in which contributions to the scheme are deducted from an employee's pay and passed by the employer to the trustees of a PENSION FUND or to an insurance company.

supermajority provisions provisions in the rules of a company that require more than the usual simple majority of its members when voting is taking place on certain motions, such as voting on a TAKEOVER BID or MERGER proposal.

supply chain a series of stages in a supply process through which a particular set of goods or services moves.

surety a sum of money held as a guarantee of something.

surrender value the sum of money that is handed over by an insurance company to the holder of a LIFE INSURANCE policy who has cancelled it before it has reached the end of the contracted period. In the early years of a life policy the surrender value is minimal, and not all life policies carry a surrender value.

suspense account a temporary account in the financial records of a company or organization that records balances to correct errors or to allow for balances that have not yet been finalized.

sweating assets a name given to the process of increasing the profits that are generated by a company's ASSETS in situations in which the RETURN on CAPITAL has been found to be inadequate. The process can involve various strategies, such as the increasing of product prices, the reduction of production costs, the reduction of costs that are related to the sales effort, the increasing of volume of sales while making use of present assets, or the reduction of the FIXED ASSETS and CURRENT ASSETS that are used to achieve the present volume of sales.

sweep facility a facility by which a bank automatically transfers a customer's funds to whichever account will bring in most INTEREST. For example, if the amount of money that a customer has deposited in a CHECKING ACCOUNT has reached a level at which more interest would be earned if the money were moved to a different type of account, under the terms of a sweep facility the bank will automatically move the money to the higher-interest account without the customer taking any action.

switching 1 the use of the money acquired from the sale of one investment in order to purchase another investment. **2** the process of exporting and importing goods through a third country where the type of currency used to pay for the goods can be exchanged into another currency that is acceptable to the seller. **3** the intervention of a country in the international currency market in order to prevent an undue outflow of its currency.

switching cost a method of making sure that a customer will be involved in additional expenditure if he or she switches to the product or service of a different supplier.

SWOT the abbreviation for STRENGTHS, WEAK-NESSES, OPPORTUNITIES AND THREATS. *See* SWOT ANALYSIS.

SWOT analysis the analysis of the internal strengths and weaknesses of a product or company and the external opportunities, such as increased consumer demand for a type of product or the failure of a firm operating in a particular field, which are open to it along with the potential threats, such as new competition or possible new legislation by government, it faces. Such an analysis is often undertaken as part of a company's business strategy.

symbol retailer *same as* VOLUNTARY RETAILER.

syndicate a group of two or more people or organizations that agree to share in a project or enterprise.

syndicated loan a LOAN that is supplied by a number of financial institutions collectively, each of the institutions providing a specified amount of money.

T

taka the standard monetary unit of Bangladesh, made up of 100 PAISA.

takeover bid an attempt by a company or individual to take over a company by making an offer to shareholders to buy their shares at a specified price in order to gain a majority of the shares and so take control of the company. See also BLACK KNIGHT, GRAY KNIGHT, WHITE KNIGHT, YELLOW KNIGHT.

tala *see* SENE.

tambala a monetary unit of Malawi, equal to one hundredth of a KWACHA.

tangible asset an ASSET that has a physical existence, such as a building or a machine. See also INTANGIBLE ASSET.

tare the weight of a container and any packaging, exclusive of its contents.

target company a company that has been targeted by an individual or company as the target of a TAKEOVER BID.

target market the segment of a market at which a firm directs its marketing thrust.

target rate of return the hoped-for rate of return on an investment.

tariff 1 a list of charges for goods or services. **2** a list of taxes or customs duties that are payable on imports or exports.

tax an assessment levied by a government to raise money for public expenses.

taxable income the amount of a person's income that is liable to taxation after the deduction of any TAX CREDITS to which the person is entitled.

tax avoidance a method of legally minimizing tax liabilities by taking maximum advantage of tax allowances and TAX RELIEF.

tax base the unit to which a tax rate is applied to find out the amount of tax payable. A person's income is a tax base, for example.

tax burden the total amount of tax that is sustained by an individual, company or organization. The tax burden includes INCOME TAX, CORPORATION TAX, INHERITANCE TAX and VALUE-ADDED TAX.

tax credit a direct reduction in the amount of taxes owed. Tax credits are allowed for expenses such as childcare.

tax-deductible referring to an amount of money that can be deducted from income or profits before the amount that is subject to tax is established.

tax evasion the process of trying to avoid paying tax by various illegal means.

tax exempt not liable to pay taxes.

tax exile a person who has a great deal of money

or who has an exceptionally high income and who lives in a TAX HAVEN so that he or she avoids the higher taxation rates of his or her original place of residence.

tax haven a country that imposes a low rate of taxes and thus attracts as residents TAX EXILES who have chosen to live there deliberately for financial gain, and also attracts companies, including multinationals, that can arrange their affairs so that at least part of their tax liability falls within the tax haven so as to minimize their tax liabilities.

tax lien a claim made by a taxing authority against a person for nonpayment of taxes. See LIEN.

tax loophole an omission or discrepancy in the tax laws that allows the nonpayment of taxes or to pay less taxes than if the loophole were not there.

tax rebate a repayment of tax paid.

tax year *same as* FISCAL YEAR.

technical analysis a method of analyzing SECURITIES by basing decisions on whether to buy or sell on their past performance. Computers are often used to carry out this function..

technical reserves the assets that are held by an insurance company against future claims or losses.

telephone selling a method of DIRECT MARKETING in which the seller of a product makes an initial contact with a potential customer. *See also* DIALING AND SMILING.

tender 1 an invitation from a prospective buyer of goods or services to prospective suppliers so that the latter may submit competing bids. **2** a method of selling shares by offering them to members of the general public who are invited to make a bid for shares, subject to a minimum bid price.

tenge the standard monetary unit of Kazakhstan.

tenor the time that has to elapse before a BILL OF EXCHANGE becomes due for payment.

term life insurance an insurance contract that pays a death benefit and is in force for a specified number of years, after which it may be renewed.

terminal value the value of an investment at the end of an investment period, taking into account the specified rate of interest.

termination discharging an employee. *See also* SEPARATION.

terms of trade a form of PRICE INDEX that indicates the ratio of a country's export process relative to its import prices.

test marketing the process of launching a new product by testing it out in a restricted geographical area or among a restricted sample of consumers so that any necessary improvements or modifications can be made before the full-scale launch takes place or so that the full-scale launch can be abandoned if the new product does not meet with approval.

thebe *see* PULA.

thin market in the STOCK MARKET, a situation in which there is a low volume of trading and there may be a wide difference between BID and ASKED prices. The opposite of a TIGHT MARKET.

third party insurance insurance that relates to someone other than the insurer or the policy-holder and occurs when there is a legal obligation to others to be taken into consideration. For example, drivers must have third-party insurance and employers must have third-party insurance to cover any injuries sustained by their employees at work.

threshold agreement an agreement entered into by management and workers that the workers' pay will be increased by a specified amount if the rate of INFLATION goes above a specified amount in a given period.

throughput time the productivity of a machine or system.

ticker tape the computerized system that relays financial information to investors worldwide.

tight market in the STOCK MARKET, a situation in which trading is active and very competitive, with only little variation between BID and ASKED prices. The opposite of a THIN MARKET.

time and motion study a form of WORK STUDY carried out to establish the best possible use of human resources and material resources in carrying out a specified activity so that maximum efficiency can be achieved. Such a study often involves the breaking down of a complex task into stages and measuring the time taken to perform each stage.

time deposit a deposit of money in an account in a commercial bank that bears INTEREST and that is deposited for a specified period.

time draft a demand for payment on a specified future date.

time sheet a document on which are recorded the tasks undertaken by a worker and the amount of time that has been spent on each task. The information provided by such a document is used not only in calculating the amount of pay that is owed to the worker but also in establishing costings.

time value the market value of an OPTION over and above its intrinsic value. It represents the value placed on the possibility that it will be worthwhile to exercise the option before it expires.

title deed a legal document that proves the ownership of land and/or property on it.

toea a monetary unit of Papua New Guinea, equivalent to one hundredth of a KINA.

tolar the standard monetary unit of Slovenia, made up of 100 stotin.

tombstone ad an advertisement announcing a NEW ISSUE of SECURITIES.

total absorption costing a method of calculating production costs that takes account not only of direct costs such as the cost of labor and the cost of materials but also other costs borne by the company, such as administrative costs.

total assets the combined amount of a company's FIXED ASSETS and CURRENT ASSETS as they are recorded in the company's BALANCE SHEET.

trade association an organization formed to represent the interests of firms that operate in the same industry.

trade credit a deferred payment system by which a supplier of goods or services allows a customer a certain period of time in which to pay for goods received.

Trade Descriptions Act (Brit) an act passed in the UK in 1968 making it a legal offence to apply a false or misleading description to goods or services.

trade discount a reduction in the usual price of goods or services to customers because they buy regularly and in bulk.

trade gap a deficit in a country's BALANCE OF PAYMENTS.

trademark a distinctive symbol, whether a

word or words or a pictorial representation, or a combination of these, that manufacturers or distributors use to identify their goods or services and to differentiate them from others.

trade price the price that is paid to a wholesaler or manufacturer by a retailer for goods that will then be sold on for a higher price, taking account of the retailer's costs.

trader a person who buys and sells SECURITIES as a profession and in order to make money for himself or herself.

trade show a gathering of the members of a particular industry at which goods and services are displayed and promoted and at which business contacts are made.

trade union the British term for a LABOR UNION.

trading buying and selling SECURITIES. See also TRADER.

trading account the section of a PROFIT AND LOSS ACCOUNT in which the cost of sales of goods is set against the sales revenue raised by the goods in order to calculate the amount of the GROSS PROFIT.

trading posts the places in the STOCK EXCHANGE where SECURITIES are traded.

trading profit the profit arising from the trading operations of a company, excluding such items as directors' fees, auditors' fees, interest, etc.

traffic management that sector of a firm responsible for planning, organizing and controlling the transportation arrangements.

tranche a part of a large sum of money.

transaction costs the costs that are associated with the process of buying and selling.

transaction exposure the extent of the risk that the cost of a transaction will alter between the date on which the transaction is carried out and the date of settlement.

transfer deed a document that is used to record the transfer of property, including shares, from one person to another.

transfer price the internal price at which raw materials, components or finished products are transacted between the divisions of a company.

traveler's check a special CHECK issued, usually for a fee, by banks and other organizations for use by travelers. Traveler's checks can easily be cashed at foreign banks

treasury bill an obligation of the US Treasury that matures in one year or less.

treasury bond a BOND issued by the US Treasury with a maturity of 10 years or more.

treasury notes an obligation of the US Treasury with a maturity of more than two years but less than 10 years.

treasury securities SECURITIES issued by the US Treasury department.

trend the general direction of the STOCK MARKET. *See also* THIN MARKET, TIGHT MARKET, BEAR MARKET, BULL MARKET.

trial balance a listing of the balances on the accounts of a company with the debit balances on one side and the credit balances on the other. This acts as an initial check on the accuracy of DOUBLE-ENTRY BOOK-KEEPING.

trinh a monetary unit of Vietnam, equal to one thousandth of a dong.

trough that period between economic recession and economic recovery.

trust an arrangement by which ASSETS are held and managed by a person or persons, the **trustee** or trustees, for the benefit of some other person or persons, called the BENEFICIARY or beneficiaries.

trustee *see* TRUST.

trust fund a fund that consists of the ASSETS belonging to a TRUST.

tugrik the standard monetary unit of Mongolia, made up of 100 MONGOS.

turnaround time the time required to carry out, complete and deliver a project.

turnkey term used to describe a project that is specifically designed for a particular client, is made, tested and ready to function before being delivered to the client.

turnover the total sales figure recorded by a

company for a specified period.

turn-round rate the total cost of a transaction on a COMMODITY market, including the commission paid to the broker and the fee payable to the CLEARING HOUSE.

two-tier tender offer a tender offer in a TAKEOVER BID in which a high initial offer is made to SHAREHOLDERS for enough SHARES to be acquired by the bidder to ensure a controlling interest in the company. This is followed by an offer to purchase the rest of the shares at a lower price. Bidders using this system do so in order to persuade shareholders to accept the initial offer quickly.

U

ultra vires (Latin) "beyond the power of." A phrase used to refer to corporate action that is outside the scope of the activities specified in its charter. Such acts are illegal.

unabsorbed costs in a production process, that part of the OVERHEAD costs not covered by the revenue it brings in when the output goes below a specified level.

unappropriated profit the portion of the profit made by a company that is neither assigned to a specific purpose nor allocated to the payment of DIVIDENDS.

unbundling an informal term used to describe the selling of many of the subsidiary companies of a CONGLOMERATE, often on takeover and sometimes with a view to paying for the takeover.

undercapitalization the state of a company that does not have the CAPITAL or reserves to support its business operations. Such a company may be in the position of making a profit but may not be able to convert its profits into cash speedily enough to discharge its financial LIABILITIES.

underperform when the value of a SECURITY rises more slowly than the overall market.

underpricing when SECURITIES are issued at a lower price than their market value.

under the counter term used to describe a transaction that is not recorded and often illegal, such as a bribe.

underwriting the acceptance by a financial organization of the financial risks involved in an enterprise on receipt of an agreed fee. For example, insurance companies are engaged in underwriting insurance risks such as fire damage to property and pay out compensation to policy-holders in the case of bona fide claims.

undifferentiated marketing a MARKETING STRATEGY that aims to exploit the widest possible market. In order to be suitable for this style of marketing, the product being marketed has to be relatively standardized with little variation.

unearned income INCOME that is not derived from employment or self-employment but is derived from the ownership of ASSETS, such as rents from properties, interest from bank accounts, DIVIDENDS from SHARES, etc.

unemployment rate the ratio of the number of people classified as unemployed to the total labor force.

unenforceable contract term used to describe a CONTRACT that may exist but is not enforceable by law. An example of this would be a verbal contract that should have later been put in writing, but wasn't.

unfair dismissal the unfair termination of an employee's employment by an employer. In order to have dismissed an employee in a fair way, the employer has to have grounds for dismissal, such as the incompetence, dishonesty, bad time-keeping, etc, of the employee or unavoidable redundancy, to have informed the employee clearly of these grounds and to have given the employee the chance to put his or her point of view of his or her defense.

unit cost the cost of a unit of production or sales in the expenditure of a company, arrived at by dividing the total production cost by the number of units involved.

unit price the price paid per unit of product or article purchased or the price charged per unit of article or product sold.

unit pricing the practice of indicating on a product pack not only the price per product pack but also the price per unit by weight, volume or pack. For example, the price per 500 grams might be shown as well as the overall cost of a joint of meat.

unit trust (Brit) a form of trust established in the UK to administrate a PORTFOLIO of securities on the STOCK EXCHANGE in which small investors can purchase units. This allows small investors to secure a wider, more diversified spread of risks than they could acquire for themselves by direct investment in a more limited number of companies.

unlimited liability the right of CREDITORS to claim every ASSET of a debtor to pay DEBTS incurred in the running of his or her business. *See also* SOLE PROPRIETOR.

unquoted company a company whose SECURITIES are not usually available to members of the public on a stock exchange.

unquoted securities SECURITIES that are not traded on a stock exchange or securities for which no price is regularly quoted.

unsecured loan a LOAN for which the borrower has no COLLATERAL security.

upstream oil and gas exploration and production. See also DOWNSTREAM.

uptick in the STOCK MARKET, when a SECURITY is sold at a higher price than the preceding transaction for the same security.

V

value added the value that is added to a company's bought-in materials and services by the company's own efforts, such as production and marketing. Value added can be evaluated by subtracting the cost of the bought-in sales and services and the sales revenue or turnover generated by the finished product or services.

value-added statement a form of accounting statement that indicates the VALUE ADDED accumulated by a company in the course of an accounting period and how this wealth has been allocated. It is allocated to employees in the form of wages and salaries, to SHAREHOLDERS and lenders in the form of DIVIDENDS and INTEREST, to the government in the form of taxation and to reinvestment in the company's business.

value-added tax (Brit) (often abbreviated to **VAT**) an INDIRECT TAX levied by the UK government on VALUE ADDED to goods or services. A value-added tax is calculated on the difference between the value of the output over the value of the inputs that are used to produce that output. The final amount of value-added tax is added to the selling price of the product and is paid by the purchaser. Some goods and services are ZERO-RATED or exempt.

value analysis a detailed examination and evaluation of a product's design or production with a view to ensuring that it is as economically and efficiently produced as possible.

value chain the chain of activities and processes by which a firm buys in materials or components, manufactures a product or creates a service, markets it and provides after-sales service.

vanilla issue the issue of a SECURITY with no unusual characteristics.

variable cost an item of business expenditure that tends to vary directly with the level of output.

variable overheads the business OVERHEADS or indirect costs that vary proportionately with the level of output. These include, for example, the cost of fuel and the cost of sales commission.

variance the difference between the budgeted levels of cost for a business activity or income from it and the actual cost or income that was achieved. In cases where the actual performance is better than that budgeted for, the variance is known as **favorable variance** or **positive variance**, and in cases where the actual performance is worse than that budgeted for, it is known as **adverse variance** or **negative variance**.

VAT the abbreviated form of VALUE-ADDED TAX.

vendor a person who sells goods or services.

venture capital CAPITAL provided either in the form of SHARE CAPITAL or LOAN CAPITAL to finance a business venture that is considered to present a higher financial RISK than usual.

venture capitalist an investor who is willing to undertake considerable financial risk in the hope of making large profits. Many new inventions and processes only become successful because of investment by venture capitalists. *See also* VULTURE CAPITALIST.

vertical disintegration the disintegration of a VERTICAL MARKETING SYSTEM as a consequence of the withdrawal of a company from one stage of the system. For example, a company may decide to withdraw from undertaking its own distribution because it is cheaper to get another company to handle this.

vertical market a market for a product that has a very limited use. The market for machinery designed to make gloves is a vertical market.

vertical marketing system a distribution system in which the relevant parties, the producers, the wholesalers and the retailers are part of a unified structure.

vertical merger a MERGER in which one firm acquires another that is in the same industry but operates within a different area. For example, a company that makes office furniture may merge with a company that manages a chain of office furniture retail outlets.

videoconferencing an electronic system that allows people in different locations to hold a discussion in which they can see each other as well as speak to each other. This reduces the need for business travel and so reduces company costs.

virement a practice that is allowed under some forms of budgetary control by which overspending under one budget expenditure heading in a company may be offset by underspending under another budget expenditure heading.

visible control a technique used in production to make any defects visible to employees. For example, a flashing light connected to an electronic sensor used to spot a defect would be a visible control.

visibles exports and imports in the form of goods rather than services, the latter being invisibles.

voice messaging the use of answering machines attached to telephones to store messages until it is possible or convenient for the recipient to receive the messages.

voluntary arrangement a system by which companies that are experiencing financial difficulties may come to an arrangement with their creditors to pay off their debts and make their own arrangements to resolve their financial difficulties rather than having to undertake a winding-up process.

voluntary retailer *or* **symbol retailer** an independent retailer who joins together with other independent retailers so that they can buy in large quantities from wholesalers at much lower prices than they could achieve without this cooperation. The groups of retailers can also benefit from promotional support and management advice as well as lower prices. The members of such a group of retailers often use a symbol or particular name to identify the group.

voluntary registration (Brit) registration for VALUE-ADDED TAX by someone whose taxable turnover does not exceed the registration threshold for value-added tax.

vostro a bank account in a UK bank held by a foreign bank.

voting shares shares in a company that give the holder of them the right to vote at the ANNUAL GENERAL MEETING of the company or at any extraordinary meetings of the company that may be called.

vulture capitalist (slang) a venture capitalist who takes over control of a new invention or process and makes more money from it than the inventor. *See also* VENTURE CAPITALIST.

W

wage differential the difference in wage rates between different groups of workers. There are several reasons for wage differentials. For example, workers in one industry may earn more than other workers in the same industry because they have particular skills or because they have greater responsibility. Also differences in productivity levels may lead to wage differentials in the same industry or in similar industries. There may also be wage differentials between one region of a country and another, perhaps reflecting levels of the supply and demand of labor and perhaps reflecting levels of prosperity and cost of living.

wage drift the tendency for the actual earnings of workers to rise faster than increases in wage rates would suggest.

wage freeze a fixing by government of wages at their existing levels in an effort to control IN-FLATION. Not only is this method of curbing IN-FLATION unpopular among workers but it is often ineffective because of money earned from overtime work and from BONUSES.

wage restraint a less drastic way of trying to control INFLATION than a WAGE FREEZE. Under a wage restraint policy, the government tries to get the unions and workers to accept only small wage increases.

waiting time the period of time during which the operators of machines, or the machines themselves, are not working because they are waiting for materials, repairs, etc.

wallflower in the STOCK MARKET, refers to a STOCK that is no longer popular with investors.

wallpaper STOCKS, SHARES, BONDS and so forth that are now worthless, usually from BANKRUPT companies.

Wall Street the name given to the New York Stock Exchange after the street in New York on which the exchange building stands. The name is also used more generally to denote the New York financial institutions generally.

war chest (slang) referring to cash reserves a company maintains to make a TAKEOVER BID or to defend itself from a hostile takeover bid.

warehouse club a retailer that sells a range of goods at substantial discounts to club members who pay an annual membership fee.

warehousing 1 the storage of goods in a warehouse. **2** the building up of a shareholding in a company before a TAKEOVER BID by purchasing small lots of shares and keeping them in the names of nominees so that the purchaser can remain anonymous.

war loan a type of government stock issued in wartime to raise funds for the war effort.

warrant a security that gives the holder the right to purchase SHARES in a company at a specified set price at a future date. Warrants are issued by companies to raise CAPITAL and they need not be included in the company's BALANCE SHEET.

warranty 1 a written assurance given by a manufacturer to replace or repair an article if this should prove faulty. Warranties usually operate for a limited time period from the time of purchase. **2** a condition included in an insurance policy, the breach of which may result in the insurer's refusal to meet a claim, even if this claim is not directly related to the breach. For example, an insurance company might include a warranty in a house contents insurance policy that certain window locks have to be used.

wash in the STOCK MARKET, where the gains equal the losses on a particular STOCK.

wasting asset a FIXED ASSET that has a finite life and becomes valueless. For example, a quarry is a wasting asset since it is without value when all the resources have been excavated from it.

wealth tax a direct tax levied by a government on a person's private assets.

whipsaw in the STOCK MARKET, to make the wrong

decision in a period of volatile price rises and falls. For example, a buyer would be whipsawed if, just after he or she had bought shares in Company A, the share price suddenly fell.

whistleblower a reference to an employee who has INSIDER knowledge of a company's illegal practices and makes this knowledge public.

white-collar worker a worker who is not a manual worker but works in the clerical, administrative or personnel departments of a company or works in one of the professions. The workers are so called because their work does not usually involve dirty conditions that debar the wearing of light clothes or necessitate the wearing of specific work clothes. In addition, their work usually demands a degree of conservatism in their clothing.

white elephant in the STOCK MARKET, refers to an unprofitable investment that nobody wants.

white elephant sale a sale held by an organization that will shortly close down.

white knight in a situation involving a TAKEOVER BID, a person or company that makes a bid that is more welcome than a previous bid that was seen as unacceptable or unwelcome in some way. If a company fears that it is going to be the target of an unwelcome takeover bid, then its directors or members may actively seek out a white knight. See also BLACK KNIGHT, GRAY KNIGHT, YELLOW KNIGHT.

whole-life policy a life-insurance policy, under the tenets of which a specified amount of money is paid on the death of the person whose life has been insured.

wholesaler a distributor who buys goods in relatively large quantities from manufacturers, stores them and sells them on in smaller quantities to RETAILERS.

windfall gain an exceptional gain that arises from an unexpected change in the financial market conditions which has helped to raise the price of a financial SECURITY, STOCK OR ASSET.

winding up bringing to an end the existence of a business; the process of selling all its ASSETS, paying CREDITORS and dividing any remaining surplus between its members.

window 1 a financial opportunity, such as a chance to invest in something profitable, which may be available only for a limited time and so should be taken advantage of. **2** a period of the day during which interbank clearances and transfers may be carried out.

window-dressing an accounting practice that aims to present the financial records of a company in the most advantageous way possible.

with dividend SHARES which give the buyer the entitlement to the next DIVIDEND payment.

withholding tax tax that is deducted at source from DIVIDEND or INTEREST payments.

with rights SHARES which give the buyer the right to buy shares in the company's RIGHTS ISSUE.

won *see* CHON.

workers' cooperative (Brit) a form of business organization that is owned and controlled by those who work in it. The concept has become more common in the UK in cases where the workers' employment prospects have been threatened and the workers have effected a workers' buy-out.

working capital the part of a company's capital that is employed in its day-to-day business operations. It consists of the difference between CURRENT ASSETS, such as cash, trading stock and money owed by debtors minus CURRENT LIABILITIES, mainly trade creditors.

work in progress goods that are still in the production or assembly process in a company. Work in progress is part of a company's INVENTORY INVESTMENT.

work study a system of techniques used to analyse human work processes. By analysing the way in which work is carried out, the system aims to improve the efficiency and effectiveness of the work methods.

work-to-rule a form of industrial action by which workers observe absolutely strictly their job descriptions and job contracts in order to cause disruption, a degree of flexibility and cooperation on the part of the workforce, outside the remit of job descriptions and contacts, being necessary if work schedules are to run smoothly.

World Bank more properly known as the International Bank for Reconstruction and Development (IBRD), this UN-controlled organization was set up in 1944. It makes long-term LOANS on favorable terms to developing countries and countries in economic need.

world investible wealth that portion of global wealth that is traded; that is to say, available for investment.

write off 1 to reduce to zero the book value of an ASSET that has become valueless, such as an expired LEASE or out-of-date machinery. **2** to reduce to zero a DEBT that is obviously not going to be discharged.

writing-down allowance (Brit) a capital allowance, introduced in 1993, available for plant and machinery used in trade in the UK. Any additions to plant and machinery are added to the WRITTEN-DOWN VALUE of assets obtained in previous years and the writing-down cost is calculated at 25 per cent of the total.

written-down value (Brit) the accounting value of a FIXED ASSET in a firm's balance sheet. This value represents the original initial cost minus any cumulative depreciation.

wrongful dismissal the dismissal of an employee which contravenes the terms of his or her employment contract.

wrongful trading the trading by a company during a period when it has no reasonable chance of avoiding insolvency or liquidation.

XYZ

XD (ex-dividend) indicates that stocks are trading without a DIVIDEND.

xu the standard monetary unit of Vietnam, equal to one hundredth of a dong.

Yankee bond foreign bonds denominated in US dollars, issued in the US by foreign banks and businesses.

Yankee market the US foreign market.

yard STOCK MARKET slang for one billion dollars.

yearling bond a BOND that is issued by a local authority and is redeemable one year after the issuing of it.

yen the standard monetary unit of Japan. *See also* RIEL, SEN.

yellow dog contract a CONTRACT between an employer and an employee in which the employee undertakes not to join a LABOR UNION. Such contracts are not enforceable in Federal courts.

yellow knight a company that first makes a TAKEOVER BID for another company but then merges with it instead. See also MERGER, BLACK NIGHT, GRAY KNIGHT, WHITE KNIGHT.

yield the return brought by any form of investment.

yuan the standard monetary unit of China, made up of 10 JIAO or 100 fen.

yuppie a slang acronym for "young urban professional", describing young, educated, career-oriented people who enjoy a high standard of living.

zaire the standard monetary unit of the Democratic Republic of Congo (formerly Zaire), being made up of 100 MAKUTA (singular form LIKUTA).

zero-based budgeting a system of budgeting that involves the preparation of a budget in a department in a company, etc, from a zero base, i.e. starting from the initial assumption that there is no commitment to spend on any activity and that every item of expenditure on every activity has to be justified. This is in contrast to the conventional budgeting system by which departmental budgets are often based on the previous year's budget with suitable updatings.

zero defects a program intended to encourage employees to aim for perfection in their work. Such programs often offer rewards for achievement.

zero-rated applied to goods and services that, although taxable, are currently subject to a tax rate of zero.

zone pricing a form of pricing system used by some companies by which their market area is divided into zones, usually those customers who live in a zone farthest from the company's headquarters or main warehouse paying more than those who live nearest.

zoning ordinance a regulation that specifies the uses to which land in a certain area may be put. For example, land set aside for residential purposes would not be available for industrial development.

Z-score a statistic that has been devised to try to summarize the susceptibility of a business to failure.

zloty the standard monetary unit of Poland, made up of 100 GROSZY.